# GENERATION
# ON HOLD

James E. Côté & Anton L. Allahar

# GENERATION ON HOLD

### Coming of Age in the Late Twentieth Century

NEW YORK UNIVERSITY PRESS

*New York and London*

NEW YORK UNIVERSITY PRESS
New York and London

Library of Congress Cataloging-in-Publication Data
Côté, James E.
Generation on hold: coming of age in the late twentieth century/
James E. Côté and Anton L. Allahar.
p.    cm.
Originally published: Toronto: Stoddart, 1994.
Includes bibliographical references and index.
ISBN 0-8147-1531-1 (cloth: alk. paper). — ISBN 0-8147-1532-X
(pbk.: alk. paper)
1. Teenagers.  2. Adolescent psychology.  I. Allahar, Anton.
II. Title.
HQ796.C8198    1995
305.23'5 — dc20              95-18151
CIP

New York University Press books are printed on acid-free paper,
and their binding materials are chosen for strength and
durability.

Cover design: Bill Douglas/The Bang

Manufactured in the United States of America

*For Joseph A. Côté, and to the memory of Jessie T. Côté. And for Anne M. Allahar and Aniisa S. Allahar. Three generations of influence who are in many ways our ghostwriters.*

# Contents

# Acknowledgments

This book is unlike most in that we do not have a great number of individuals to acknowledge. In essence, however, there are three groups that are worth mentioning. First, and most generally, are our students who, over the years, have struggled to come of age in advanced industrial society, and have encountered all the triumphs and setbacks that such a process entails. We have taught them as we have learned from them. Second, we would like to thank those colleagues who, through their negativity, made the writing of the book even more meaningful. And third, our thanks are extended to Michael Carroll and Deborah Viets and the very professional and supportive staff of Stoddart Publishing, who were experienced enough to recognize the differences in expertise between writers and editors and, with a minimum of ego-bruising, greatly enhanced the process of communicating our ideas to our audiences.

# Introduction

## A BRIEF HISTORY OF YOUTH

Throughout history adults have expressed concerns about the members of their community who were on the verge of coming of age. Records of complaints about recalcitrant youth date as far back as the eighth century b.c. when the Greek poet Hesiod warned that he saw no future if society depended "on the frivolous youth of today, for certainly all youth are reckless beyond words."[1] Similar laments can be found in other writings through the ages, including those of William Shakespeare and George Bernard Shaw. In *The Winter's Tale*, Shakespeare crafted the Shepherd who wished that youth could be bypassed because the young do nothing other than "getting wenches with child, wronging the ancientry, stealing, fighting."[2] And Shaw complained that youth was wasted on the young. Regardless of how accurate such assessments were of this period of life, they still carry a certain resonance, as does Hesiod's belief that when he was young, he was "taught to be discreet and respectful of elders, but the present youth are exceedingly wise and impatient of restraint."

What do we make of this recurrent view of young people? Most obviously, it appears that coming of age is often associated with tensions between neophyte and adult members of societies. This tension varies according to one's culture, and within specific cultures, and tensions run higher during certain periods of history.[3]

Let us consider for a moment the commonsense view of youth that might be taken by the average person in contemporary Western society. Such a person might feel that when young people act immaturely, they must be inherently that way, or that when they do not seem to be able to handle responsibilities, there must be something about them that makes them irresponsible. On the basis of common sense, members of the general public often conclude that these supposedly immature and irresponsible individuals must be closely watched and regulated by adult authorities.

The commonsense view of adolescence and youth casts this period of life as a natural and necessary stage of development. Young people are believed to be biologically and emotionally immature and therefore unsuited to be admitted to society as full-fledged members. Many people feel that if adolescents do not accept the conditions of this phase of the life cycle, there must be something wrong with them, something that makes them unable to control themselves and accept what everyone else takes for granted — the inevitability of a slow and prolonged coming of age. The general public tends to believe that adolescence is as inevitable as old age and death. As we shall see, several social scientific perspectives reflect this commonsense view of young people.

The views we have just discussed are specific to contemporary Western societies. Before the 20th century young people in Western societies were thought of quite differently, primarily because the sharp distinction between adulthood and adolescence did not exist. Under the right circumstances teenagers could assume many adult roles without interference: they could work, marry, and join the military.[4] In fact, the notion of adolescence as a distinct stage of life was introduced by social scientists at the turn of the century to name what was defined as a "problem" created by young people.[5] The deviance associated with adolescence in industrial society was believed to be an inevitable part of growing up. According to this view, which persists today, adolescents are prone to uncontrollable biological impulses. Consequently, adolescence is seen as a rather distasteful and tempestuous stage through which everyone must pass. It is tolerated because of the belief that during this period of storm and stress we learn how to manage our impulses and achieve a balance between tumultuous and conflicting emotional states. Many adults maintain that it is best to leave young people in turmoil because their moodiness has biological roots.[6]

This view of adolescence, which was formally developed by the psychologist G. Stanley Hall, has informed much theorizing about the young, particularly among psychologists and psychiatrists. Many of Hall's assumptions are still part of the psychological and psychiatric stock of knowledge. His assumptions persist even though many studies have shown that adolescent turmoil is not universal to all cultures and therefore cannot be an inevitable part of human development.[7] Still, those social scientists who believe human behavior is strongly influenced by genetic factors continue to favor biological views of adolescence. This position belongs to the "nature" side of the nature-versus-nurture debate — the great debate of 20th-century social science in which the relative importance of genetic and environmental causes of behavior are contested. The fact that this larger controversy is relevant to the study of adolescence complicates matters because the controversy has serious political implications.[8]

The nurture view, widely embraced by anthropologists and sociologists, holds that adolescence and its concomitant difficulties are a product of certain cultural conditions. This argument was first advanced by Margaret Mead in her pioneering study *Coming of Age in Samoa.*[9] Since the 1920s, when Mead carried out her study of a non-Western culture, considerable historical and cross-cultural evidence suggests that the phenomenon of adolescence is specific to certain cultures and that its structure changes over time in the cultures where it exists.[10]

This evidence indicates that mainstream societal expectations form the basis of how coming of age is structured in a given culture, and therefore even whether or not periods akin to Western adolescence are found. Moreover, when such periods emerge, a smooth transition to adulthood depends upon whether or not adults provide a supportive and welcoming environment. Mead's study suggests that several conditions are important to produce a coming of age that is relatively stress-free.[11] She contends that the adult community should provide a set of consistent beliefs and a clear role for the young person to play as he or she enters adulthood. In the face of inconsistent beliefs and ambiguous roles, young people experience conflicts that can precipitate the difficulties to which Hall and others have referred.

Mead realized that the conditions found in small, homogeneous societies cannot be easily replicated in large, heterogeneous ones. The key difference between her Samoan adolescents and those in Western societies is the number of career and religious choices available to them, and hence the number of decisions they must make. Mead suggested that adolescents in Western societies should receive an "education for choice," which would teach them that the notion of limitless choice is an illusion, as well as emphasizing the importance of critical thinking, the necessity of tolerance, and the hazards of prejudice.[12] In spite of their simplicity, we can take from Mead's insights a sense of what coming of age can be like if the process is appropriately structured. Too often it is not; consequently, the young do not receive an adequate education for choice.

## YOUTH IN THE PRESENT ERA

Most social scientists agree that the advent of industrial society heralded a dramatic change in terms of how young people came of age. Increasingly, the teen years became a period of dependency and relative leisure, a phenomenon that resulted in new tensions between adults and youths.[13] We argue in this book that something new has happened to the way young people come of age as we have moved into the era of advanced industrial society. Changes in the occupational and educational structures of industrial society appear to be affecting the coming-of-age process in several ways. As we enter the mid-1990s, these changes are becoming more obvious and public attention is again turning to the young members of society, prompted in part by collective outbursts in the streets and escalating troubles in schools. However, these outbursts do not appear to be part of a movement to create a new and better society as was the case during the 1960s, the most recent period of widespread youth dissent. Rather, we contend that the dissent we are now witnessing is a manifestation of the frustration and alienation felt by a disenfranchised and economically manipulated group. The rioting in major Western cities, the growing necessity for armed guards in violence-prone high schools where students carry weapons, the formation of violent gangs, even in small towns, high levels of un- and underemployment, epidemic levels of suicide, and mindless consumerism are all part of the same problem that leaves many young people aimlessly groping to come of age in the 1990s.

Surprisingly, in spite of their ongoing fascination with young people's antics, social scientists have expressed little interest recently in the coming-of-age phenomenon. The press has been much more attuned to these issues and in a sense has scooped academics on these stories. As informative as journalists' reports are, they have not presented a comprehensive overview and diagnosis of the problems facing the young in the 1990s. Our book attempts to fill this gap and uses a methodology that integrates several social scientific perspectives.

This book is about the changing circumstances confronting young people as they grow up and try to come of age in advanced industrial societies. These circumstances include the long wait adolescents must face between the time when they become physically mature and when they are considered to be socially mature, or "adult." The delay is characterized by economic and social marginality; sequestration into age-segregated groups, and extended financial and emotional dependence on parents. The young are also subject to manipulation and control by a variety of groups formed by adults who are out to protect their own interests.

Our multifaceted argument reflects the complex circumstances facing people as they come of age. It can be broken down roughly as follows:

▶ First, the prolonged period we call adolescence and youth resulted from industrialization and the legislation developed to stabilize industrial societies, such as child labor laws and compulsory education.

▶ Second, we propose that as we moved into the most recent phase of industrial capitalism, which began in the 1950s, the coming-of-age process has become even longer, primarily because the labor of adolescents and youth is no longer needed, except in service industries. Consequently, young people have lost a "franchise." Now they participate less in the labor force, and when they do, it is in a more subservient manner. Accordingly, fewer young people have the full rights and privileges of citizenship, and they must wait longer before they are fully recognized as adults. In addition to not being able to make a meaningful contribution to the economy, young people have been forced to remain in school longer, where they are under the watchful eye of massive educational bureaucracies.

▶ Third, young people have been targeted as consumers rather than as producers by the service, leisure, information, and high-technology sectors of the advanced industrial economy. In other words, young people have increasingly been targeted as consumers of "leisure industries" (e.g., media and music) and "identity industries" (e.g., fashion and education).

▶ Fourth, we submit that these leisure and identity industries have merged to create a culture in which coming of age involves allying oneself with one of these forces — for example, adopting one of the images manufactured by the leisure industries, or predicating an identity on the credentials conferred by the educational system.

▶ Fifth, we contend that many young people today face a situation where conflict, chaos, and confusion underlie a superficial harmony. Developing a viable adult identity has become an increasingly tenuous process for those coming of age because many of the identities they are sold by adult profiteers are illusory and fleeting. Consequently, we believe that there is an epidemic of socially produced identity crises in advanced industrial societies.

▶ Finally, the above forces have combined to create a paradoxical situation. Numerous influences are directed at the disenfranchised young to "manufacture their consent" as consumers of adult-produced identities and self-images. Although these consent-manufacturing forces have been successful, there are signs that they are becoming ineffective, and the overall result is a manufacture of dissent. The latter phenomenon is behind the collective outbursts and the epidemic of identity crises to which we have alluded, as well as many of the liabilities of youth we go on to discuss.

Throughout this book, we draw on the writings of other social scientists whose commentaries on adolescence and youth have dealt with the economics and history of education, youth unemployment and crime, family structure, and personal aspirations. Our aim, however, is to go beyond such commentaries, which generally focus on one isolated aspect of the coming-of-age process to the exclusion of others. We have attempted to present a multifaceted interpretation of the problems associated with this process. In addition to diagnosing the problems, we undertake the risky task of recommending solutions. Our approach is, therefore, interdisciplinary: we draw freely from anthropology, demography, history, psychology, psychoanalysis, economics, and sociology in our attempt to understand the crisis youth face today and the implications that this crisis holds for society at large.

In some respects, specific details of our study are not new, for there are now well over 5,000 books dealing with various aspects of youth and adolescence. Those books, however, appear to have had little impact on the problems we identify and discuss. We hope that this book will reach the audiences that need to know what is happening to the young person's world: youths themselves, their parents, teachers, community leaders, educational policy-makers, and even educational funding agencies.

Part One

---

# The Prolongation
# of Youth

---

*A* number of forces have coalesced to set in motion a prolongation of adolescence and youth that continues today. In order to understand how young people come of age in advanced industrial societies, we need to examine these forces and consider the impact of the prolongation of youth.

▶ *Chapter 1 traces the history of the concept of adolescence as it has been developed and used by social scientists. It would appear that an understanding of youth has been constructed by some social scientists, in part to engineer a consensus about the true nature of this period of life. By examining the different perspectives social scientists assume with regard to youth, we can identify the causes of certain changes in coming-of-age processes.*

▶ *Social and economic trends that determine the opportunities and quality of life available to young people are explored in chapter 2. When we interpret the statistics that reflect these trends, we find that contrary to the widely held belief that youth is the best time of one's life, young people now constitute one of the most disadvantaged and vulnerable groups of the entire population. Furthermore, in North America, the circumstances facing many young people have worsened*

3

*dramatically in the past several decades as we have moved from an industrial to an advanced industrial society. Young people have been disenfranchised as a result of this transition.*

▶ *Finally, taking our cue from the sociological implications of the first two chapters, in chapter 3 we develop a model of the social-psychological mechanisms used to manipulate young persons. We note that one way to control people is to regulate the way they define themselves and their place in the world. We argue that the psychological and social bases of their sense of identity have been rendered tenuous by social changes associated with contemporary society and that dominant interests have capitalized on this vulnerability in numerous ways. This identity manipulation, as we call it, is illustrated by showing how the conceptions of masculinity and femininity are shaped and exploited by various interest groups, and how this exploitation has made the passage from adolescence to adulthood hazardous.*

# 1

----

# The Discovery of Youth

----

**W**hile the idea of youth as a distinct stage of life was "discovered" by G. Stanley Hall at the beginning of the 20th century, as we approach the 21st century, the controversy continues as to what was actually discovered. In an old Hindu folktale about three blind men and an elephant, we see that how something is described depends in part on one's position in relation to the thing. Similarly, the positions social scientists take regarding youth are generally divided in terms of whether they view human behavior as biologically or socially determined. Although most social scientists studying adolescence do not explicitly speak of nature versus nurture, often their underlying assumptions reflect one of the contrasting positions.

## NATURE: ADOLESCENCE AS A PRODUCT OF BIOLOGY

To help young people deal with their emotional problems, a veritable army of psychologists and psychiatrists is employed either by the state or by wealthy parents. In fact, many of these helping professionals only have contact with emotionally disturbed young persons. This would explain why many of them tend to think of all young people as emotionally unstable.[1] Focusing on either the psychological or the psychiatric perspectives carries the risk of overestimating the extent to which adolescence and youth intrinsically represent periods of intense emotional distress.

Both the psychological and psychiatric views concentrate on the inner workings of the individual. In doing so they tend to overlook the extent to which individuals are socially influenced. According to the psychiatric and psychological perspectives, adolescence and youth are periods when certain developmental changes *must* occur if the individual is to become a healthy adult. If such changes do not take place, both views advocate adjusting the individual to make the changes happen. While psychiatrists and psychologists acknowledge the role environmental or social influences play in shaping adolescents' behavior, they rarely undertake detailed analyses of these factors.

## Psychological Views: Storm and Stress

G. Stanley Hall's view that adolescence is a universal stage of development *and* that it is characterized by storm and stress influenced psychology for decades. As we saw, however, anthropological evidence contradicted the storm and stress assertion, so many psychologists revised their views and began to acknowledge the important role played by culture in shaping behaviors during adolescence. Current psychological views continue to see adolescence as a development stage, or at least as a period in which stages of cognitive and emotional development take place. Until quite recently, however, the role played by culture in shaping adolescent cognition and emotion has been given lip service, so the attention in psychology has been on changes within the adolescent rather than on the role of culture in bringing about these changes.[2]

David Proefrock, a psychologist himself, has critically examined the history of the psychological model of adolescence and argues that the primary focus on the individual has had some unfortunate consequences. For example, the work of some psychologists has had the effect of shaping the nature of this period of development.[3] Based on views advanced by G. Stanley Hall in *Adolescence* (1904), Proefrock argues that the psychopathology attributed to adolescence was used to legitimate the juvenile justice system in the United States and the suspension of rights imposed by that system. According to current American law, if a case can be made that there is something wrong with an individual, especially if that person is believed not to be responsible for his or her behavior, custody and treatment are justified, even if the behavior is a mere so-called status offense.[4] Indeed, psychologist Gary Melton notes that "limitations on adolescents' rights have been premised on unsupportable assumptions about adolescents' competence as decision makers, [and] the vulnerability of adolescents."[5]

Proefrock warns of the dangers of the psychological position if taken to the extreme. He reminds us "that the developmental period of adolescence does not exist outside of the social factors which caused its emergence," and we are therefore "in danger of making attributions to the adolescent which exist because of social conditions. These attributions . . . are not . . . intrinsic to the persons themselves. They are intrinsic to the person living under a particular set of societal constraints and dictates."[6] This insight is unfortunately ignored by many clinical and research psychologists, as well as by many of those in the other helping professions.

This said, it is important to acknowledge that psychologists are on the "front line" in terms of dealing with the problems young people face and working on a one-to-one basis they can do very little to alter the social circumstances facing this group as a whole. The only recourse they have is to assist the young in developing coping skills. On these grounds, we sympathize with the task of psychologists.

Still, it is difficult to condone helping young people to "cope" by mystifying them about the source of their problems and citing the young people in question as the primary cause of these problems. While some individual young people must shoulder the blame for their difficulties, it must, nevertheless, be recognized that as a *group*, young people share common circumstances that are not their fault.

Psychologists can help many youths out of desperate straits and have helped us understand many of the inner processes affecting the behavior of the young. However, to the extent that the psychological perspective ignores or denies evidence that the young are disadvantaged in certain ways, it tends to blame them for circumstances of which they may be the actual victims.[7]

## Psychiatric Views: A Biological Affliction

Psychiatrists share many of the assumptions associated with the psychological view of coming of age. However, because of their greater investment in biological concepts, many psychiatrists have an even more exaggerated tendency to see young people as "afflicted" with the so-called condition of adolescence. In fact, as we see, there is a tendency in psychiatry to see adolescence itself as a disorder with various sets of symptoms. This view ignores the extent to which adolescence is a product of culture and the fact that behavioral disturbances among adolescents are a response to problems within the culture.

In fairness to some psychiatrists, especially those who address the cultural relativity of adolescence, we should point out that there is a movement in the field that recognizes that adolescence is largely a cultural phenomenon, not a biological one. Unfortunately, this movement is not uniform and many of those who introduce this idea into their writings do not adequately articulate how the culture or social environment is implicated in adolescent difficulties. Instead, they tend to moralize about the evils of adolescent behavior. We will first discuss the traditional psychiatric view of adolescence and then examine how this has changed.

The traditional psychiatric view is predicated on biology and may be summarized as advocating that young people hang on until their "condition" subsides. Take for example the following recommendation made by D. W. Winnicott in *Adolescent Psychiatry*, a leading psychiatric publication:

There exists one real *cure for adolescence,* and only one, and this cannot be of interest to the boy or girl who is in the thoes. *The cure for adolescence belongs to the passage of time and to the gradual maturation process;* these together do in the end result in the emergence of the adult person. This process cannot be hurried or slowed up, though indeed it can be broken into and destroyed, or it can wither up from within, in psychiatric illness.[8]

Such a statement appears naive when considered in relation to the more contemporary social scientific perspectives we examine in this book. Yet, such views apparently informed psychiatric practice just 20 years ago and therefore guided the process of drafting social policies affecting young people. More incredible still is Winnicott's statement, which holds that the crucial thing to be recognized "is the fact that the adolescent boy and girl do not want to be understood. Adults must hide among themselves what they come to understand of adolescence."[9] These patronizing remarks do not reveal the type of compassion one would expect in a doctor-patient relationship, and while we use Winnicott as an example, other psychiatrists share the approach he uses to understand and deal with adolescents.

Some psychiatrists presume that the experiences of their young patients speak for the experience of all adolescents in all times and places. For example, Winnicott also wrote that "adolescence is something that we have always with us."[10] And Dana Farnsworth has stated that "the needs of a young person during adolescence have probably changed little over the centuries."[11]

Our intention here is not to embarrass individual writers, but to point out how fatuous some experts can be when there are no checks against their authority. Fortunately, these views held by members of the psychiatric profession have been challenged by social scientists who have examined adolescence and youth from historical and cross-cultural perspectives. For example, Robert Hill and J. Dennis Fortenberry recently wrote about psychiatrists' tendency to pathologize adolescence and concluded that adolescence "is neither a disease nor an epidemic." Indeed, they go on to argue that viewing adolescence as an age-based pathological condition serves to mask social factors that threaten well-being in advanced societies. They contend that this view is based on the stereotype of young people that has emerged in Western societies and that by looking only for disorders inherent in the young person, "adolescent medicine specialties may unintentionally draw attention away from more important bases of youth morbidity and mortality: racism, the juvenilization of poverty, underemployment, inadequate education and declining per-capita resources for dependent children and youth."[12]

The tendency of psychiatrists to see the world in terms of pathologies has been the subject of jokes and clichés for some time. The fact that it persists is disturbing, but it also suggests something about a hidden agenda of this profession and of dominant interests in society. Perhaps not coincidentally, the tendency to see certain behavior as pathological serves as a very effective method of establishing a clientele (for psychiatrists) and for maintaining the status quo (for dominant interests). For example, some psychiatrists speak in terms of "legitimate treatment prospect[s]."[13] Most have a vested interest in maintaining their legitimacy as practicing a medical science, although many of their criteria are soft by scientific standards. Psychiatrists have perhaps been too willing to do the bidding for dominant interests in society. Warren Gadpaille touches on these points in an introspective passage directed at other psychiatrists. He submits that his colleagues must ask themselves the following questions about their role: "Are they agents of the adolescents, of the adolescents' family, or of society? To what extent are these roles separable? Can psychiatrists function in a broader-than-individual therapeutic context without subordinating adolescents' interests to those of family or society."[14]

While there seems to be a growing awareness of the questions raised by Gadpaille here, we do not believe that all practicing psychiatrists have faced them. Indeed, as a number of sociologists have suggested, all of the helping professions can be seen as part of a massive bureaucratic mechanism whose mandate is, in part, to control young people. In order to justify restricting youths, an ideology of treatment (the medical model) has been created and it has the full force and legitimacy of science, medicine, and the state. Normal behavior is defined in terms of conformity or adjustment to the status quo. If one does not accept the conditions set out by the status quo, one is deemed maladjusted and in need of rehabilitation.

The problem with this approach is that it does not account for the possibility that the source of the difficulty lies within society and not the individual. If we consider the possibility that the socioeconomic relations of a society create many mental difficulties and that the psychiatric profession is incapable of detecting this because of its neglect of social environments and its focus on biology, then psychiatrists might be really forcing youths to adjust to an untenable set of circumstances. Or, at the very least, they might be forcing them to make adjustments that actually hinder or retard their development.[15] As argued below, this latter possibility appears to be what happens to many young people who rebel against the unnatural constraints placed on them. But for the adolescent, there is a bind in that the rebellion is taken as a further indication of maladjustment, as a result of which more intensive treatment is recommended, which causes further rebellion, and so on.

A number of social scientists have commented on the self-serving tendency in adolescent psychiatry. For example, Norman Sprinthall and W. Andrew Collins are critical of the diagnostic categories covering adolescent behavior that have proliferated with a recent edition of the *Diagnostic and Statistical Manual (DSM) III*. They argue that "the category system is so broad in scope that virtually all aspects of adolescent behavior that deviate in any way from the normative can be labelled as mental disease."[16] In the journal *The Clinical Psychologist*, Norman Garmezy charges that this classification system is not only self-serving but has a negative impact on young people because their changes and adjustments are now defined as mental disorders. Indeed, the original diagnostic manual from 1952 cited only 60 disorders, while the 1980 version cites 230 disorders.[17] As Sprinthall and Collins note:

> What DSMIII does, then, is to take a rather common difficulty in adolescence — academic underachievement, for example — and transform the problem into a form of mental illness. And then following diagnosis comes a treatment recommendation — referral to a medically trained psychiatrist. When we realize that academic underachievement for high school males is extremely common (estimates run as high as 30 to 40%), then we see that DSMIII has turned a common phenomenon of adolescence into a psychiatrically defined illness, complete with label, code number, and treatment recommendation.[18]

Included in the pathologies that psychiatrists see in adolescents are such things as:

▶ Specific reading disorder

▶ Shyness disorder

▶ Oppositional disorder

▶ Emancipation disorder of adolescence or early adult life

▶ Adolescent adjustment disorder

▶ Identity disorder

▶ Specific academic or work disorder

But, let us examine just what constitutes such pathologies. As an example, we will focus on the "specific academic or work disorder." Here we find what can reasonably be considered as a set of normal problems faced by those who are forced to participate in a system that is alienating and unrewarding, as is the case with much of the public educational system and most of the workplace. The "essential features" of this "mental disorder" are:

> Severe stress interfering significantly with any of the following academic or work tasks and manifested by: Anxiety related to examinations or other tests[;] Inability to

write papers, prepare reports, or perform in studio arts activities[;] Difficulty in concentration on studies or work[;] Avoidance of studying or work that does not seem to be under conscious control[;] Distress not present when the person is not thinking about the academic or work task . . .[19]

Such a condition can describe the experiences of most students at one time or another. But surely the pressures of school systems that *demand* regimented conformity and regurgitation and which do not take into account the feelings or needs of students can be held accountable for these experiences.

## Problems with Nature Approaches

Both the psychological and psychiatric perspectives represent potent forces in contemporary Western societies, and both have a vested interest in maintaining the view that the problems of young people can be addressed by "adjusting" them, rather than by changing society. Moreover, policy-makers want to hear this because making significant social reforms is not to their advantage since it would require taking initiatives that act against dominant interests; instead they stick with the bureaucratic ritualism that passes for policy-making. The establishment protects dominant political and economic interests by turning back the frustrations experienced by youths on them rather than acknowledging their sources in the society. The ultimate solution to many of the problems facing the young lies with altering the social circumstances to which they are subjected, not with merely treating the casualties of these circumstances, as we will show by examining various sociological perspectives.

As we also demonstrate, historical changes in the way the transition from childhood to adulthood has been structured in Western culture prove that there simply is no *one* way that human beings come of age. Historical variation in the structure of adolescence indicates that, despite the biological changes that take place during and following puberty, coming of age is determined by culture more than by the biological makeup of the individual.[20] Consequently, it is less fruitful to examine the individual in order to understand the causes of what happens during the coming-of-age period than it is to look at how a culture shapes an individual and how it leads that person to develop certain attributes and behavior instead of others.

Aside from these concerns, the truth is that when subjected to scientific tests, the common biological assumptions regarding adolescence have proven to be faulty. For example, after their close review of psychological literature based on the biological approach, Anne Petersen and Brandon Taylor conclude that "we have been overestimating the significance of biological factors because of the difficulty of dealing with some problems associated with adolescence. We tend misguidedly to equate 'biological' with 'immutable.'"[21] In fact, they argue that no evidence currently exists that behaviors associated with delinquency and rebellion are biologically determined. Referring to the belief that hormones are primarily responsible for emotional turmoil among adolescents, Jeanne Brooks-Gunn and Michelle Warren note that in the empirical literature, "hormone-affect associations, when found . . . are small. . . . No direct effects of pubertal status were found."[22] In their own study of the negative affect of 100 10- to 14-year-old females, Brooks-Gunn and Warren found that "endocrine system factors . . . accounted for no more than 4% of variance in negative emotional expression . . . [while] social factors accounted for more variance (8% and 18% for depressive and aggressive affect, respectively) than biological factors." They concluded from these findings that "hormonal activation effects in humans may not be large . . . and may be overshadowed by environmental events."[23]

Researchers who continue to look for the elusive connection between biological factors and adolescent behavior, such as the "hormone-delinquency link,"[24] rely on considerable argumentation and statistical manipulation to make their point. Even with these vigorous efforts, no one has been able to demonstrate statistically that biological variables are *more* important than social ones.[25] At best, biological effects are either minor or indirect in that they are mediated by culture. While they may have had more of a *direct* effect on behavior early in human evolution, humans have long since become an acculturated species for which instincts have become quite weakened and diffused.[26] Biological influences now appear to be indirect in the sense that cultures have the capacity both to intensify and neutralize them. As Sprinthall and Collins argue, "the effects of the primary physical changes of adolescence are *socially mediated* by the reactions of self and others."[27] Accordingly, the adolescent's self-image and self-esteem "are determined by sociocultural standards, norms, and expectations about physical characteristics that are widely held in a society or culture."

Complicating matters further is the fact that behind many biological assumptions lies an equating of puberty with adolescence. But, strictly speaking, the term *puberty* refers to biological changes that occur during the early teen years or what is now called early adolescence. As we mentioned, it has been proven that the behavioral correlates of puberty are nonexistent, indirect, or minor. Thus, the belief in a biological inferiority among those coming of age is unjust, insofar as society's treatment of them has been based on a false belief that the determinants of their behavior are biological rather than social.

In any event, our concern is not primarily with puberty or early adolescence, but with the later teens and early twenties, when coming of age is actually supposed to take place. These older age groups are clearly past puberty, so to assert that their undesirable behavior stems from a hormonal balance is dubious. Clearly, the argument that individuals in their late teens and twenties are biologically immature does not justify the suspension of their rights, yet this is what is increasingly happening as adolescence and youth have become more prolonged.[28]

For centuries, individuals in their teen years were seen to be capable of mature and responsible behavior, including beginning their own families. Moreover, before the present century, puberty occurred at a later age than it does today.

How is it then that we now impute less maturity to individuals of this age? Has something changed to make them constitutionally more immature, despite accelerated biological development? If so, what has changed?

## NURTURE: ADOLESCENCE AS A PRODUCT OF CULTURE

Sociologists tend to view adolescence as a product of social expectations associated with a given culture.[29] In spite of this shared assumption, divergencies among sociological views are often great, so it is useful to separate the sociological perspectives with respect to the influences that are most important in structuring coming-of-age processes. All those working in the field believe that adolescence and youth are institutions imposed on those coming of age by forces beyond their control. The differences among the perspectives lie in how this imposition is explained — why it is there and whether or not it is justified.

### Functionalist Views: Industrialization

According to the functionalist view, youth and adolescence are in a sense a function of the social change associated with industrialization. Functionalists note that the human life cycle in Western culture has become increasingly differentiated, owing largely to industrialization.[30] In particular, the period between childhood and adulthood has changed significantly. Three factors are seen to have contributed to this differentiation. The first two can be considered side effects of early industrialization, and the third a product of advanced industrialization.

First, because of improvements in nutrition, sanitation, and health care, the onset of puberty now takes place some four years earlier than it did in 1850.[31] In fact, since the 1850s, puberty has begun about one year earlier for every 25 years of improvement in these areas. In the present era, the average age for the onset of puberty is about 12 for females and 14 for males.[32] During the 1850s these figures would have been about 16 and 18, respectively.

Second, industrialization has made it less necessary for the family unit to rely on the labor of the young, beginning first with children and then with teens. Young people have gone from being central to agricultural economies to being marginal to industrial economies; and they have gone from being economic assets to being economic liabilities for their families. Of course, they are not overtly recognized as economic liabilities by most parents, but this is due mainly to the ideologies and institutions that have sprung up to justify the new social positions of the young. These ideologies include the importance of protecting the young from the evils and hardships of the adult world; the institutions include the education system and various government agencies entrusted with enforcing this separation from the adult world.

These two side effects of industrialization have prolonged adolescence at both boundaries: young people become sexually mature and develop cognitive capacities earlier, but they remain dependent much longer on their parents (and parental surrogates, such as schools). Thus, we have a situation of an enforced and prolonged dependency that simply did not exist prior to the development of industrialization. Prior to industrialization, the onset of puberty coincided with a loosening of parental ties.[33] Even when young people remained in their parents' homes, they were not granted a life-style of relative leisure, as is now the case; rather they were expected to contribute their labor or earnings to the household.

The third factor influencing the way we come of age has been produced by the conditions of advanced industrial society. The latter term is often used to designate the shift from a primary manufacturing base in the economy to a large service base, whereby a growing segment of the workforce produces "intangibles" rather than tangible manufactured goods.[34] The intangibles include the basic "catering" role of the service economy (e.g., the fast-food industry, transportation, and sales); the "facilitating" role of the information economy (e.g., banking, telecommunications); and the "steering" role of the high-technology economy (e.g., computer programming, education).

The expanding service economy affects the way people come of age in the sense that it induces them to strive for the upper-level facilitating and steering jobs, as we have called them, in order to escape the monotony of working as a waiter or salesperson. In order to move up the ladder, young people must obtain higher educational credentials. However, many get stuck at the bottom of the ladder, remaining in the lowest level "catering" positions, despite having acquired postsecondary credentials by studying well into their 20s. As a result, their aspirations go unrealized and they feel disappointed because they are unable to attain the level of independence one usually associates with adulthood. In other words, adolescence has been prolonged even further for many individuals. We have previously made a link between its prolongation and the entrenchment of the industrial economy. With the entrenchment of the *advanced* industrial economy in the last half of this century, and the rise of postsecondary education as a standard stage in career development, the phase of life referred to as youth became part of social scientific terminology.[35]

There is considerable evidence to support the functionalist view of adolescence. As noted earlier, many scholars argue that the notion of adolescence as a distinct stage of life is a relatively recent invention. As Roy Baumeister and Dianne Tice argue, before 1800 "Americans did not think of youth as a period of personal indecision, awkwardness and uncertainty, or passive and helpless vulnerability. Rather, the general attitude was that puberty meant the young person was ready and able to do an adult's share (or almost) of work around the farm, shop, or house."[36] Similarly, Wendell Cultice writes that:

> In a sense, there were no teenagers in early America. That is, there was no easily identifiable group of young people of certain ages who acted, dressed, and spoke in ways that were markedly different from those of other age groups. It was not uncommon for boys and girls to be married at age 16 or younger, and as young married people, they were then expected to act as adults. Such expectations included military service for the males.[37]

If we accept this view of adolescence as a relatively recent phenomenon, what are the implications for how the contemporary adolescent and youth should be viewed? This is neither a flippant question, nor an easy one to answer. For, despite attempts to demarcate adolescence and childhood, it is not clear when childhood ends and adolescence begins. For example, puberty is not a homogenous process; rather it includes numerous stages of growth.[38] Even the age ranges that mark the onset of puberty are misleading. Raymond Montemayor and Daniel Flannery recently concluded that "advances in the study of puberty indicate that pubertal change begins much earlier than previously thought and is a long-term gradual process."[39] Thus, many people thought of as children have already begun the transition toward adulthood.

The point here is that any attempt to firmly establish these age periods is arbitrary and does more to nurture a sense of certainty about the state of the world than it does to neatly characterize what may actually be happening. Many people see adolescence as corresponding to the teen years, at least to age 18. However, for the legal establishment in the United States adolescence "begins at 16 years of age and ends at 21."[40]

The historical relativity of adolescence is now common knowledge in many of the social sciences. Sprinthall and Collins, who deal with this matter throughout their textbook, *Adolescent Psychology: A Developmental View*, address the issue of the social construction of both childhood and adolescence. They contend that "until adults recognized and allowed childhood to emerge, it hardly existed. For long centuries it was thought that as soon as a child reached the age of six or seven, the child was ready to be trained as an adult. Children were considered as little more than midget-sized adults." There was no firm age-graded distinction among people. Children "worked alongside adults in the fields, they fought adult wars, they worked in the mines, and with the coming of industrialization they worked from dusk to dawn in the factories."[41]

Sprinthall and Collins also note the differentiation in the life cycle that began with the onset of industrialization:

Once childhood was discovered, a whole series of changes followed. . . . What was true for the discovery of childhood in the last century has been the case for adolescence in this century. . . . In the last half of the twentieth century we are beginning to witness some changes in how adolescents are treated by adult society, similar to the changes experienced by juveniles in the nineteenth century.[42]

Like many other social scientists, these authors attribute the emergence of childhood and adolescence largely to the perceived need to educate the young and to the child protection movement that sought to codify these concerns into laws. Usually initiated by reformers, some of whom claimed to be intent on protecting the young from various imagined evils, primary schools were established first, institutionalizing childhood and cementing people's conceptions of this age period. More recently secondary schools were established, with the same results for this age period.

While there is obviously much that is useful and convincing in the functionalist perspective, this view of society has been criticized for being too descriptive and assuming too much of a natural evolution of society. Critics feel that the functionalist view assumes too much inevitability in the social order and social change. As we will see, other sociologists look to conscious, human action in shaping the social order and directing social change, and this action is often seen to be self-interested in a way that allows some groups to benefit at the expense of others.

## Subcultural Views: The Peer Group

Another sociological view focuses on the collective reactions of young people in industrial societies who do not find meaning in their lives because of their marginalization from adult society.[43] Sociologists who advocate this perspective study cliques and subcultures that develop to fill the void created by the incompleteness and meaninglessness of the roles granted young people by adults. Because they are not allowed to participate fully in adult culture, youths develop their own culture in an attempt to find a more meaningful identity.[44]

This becomes increasingly the case the more marginalized a young person is in terms of race and social class background. The more mainstream adult culture ignores the young, the more youth subcultures will reject adult culture and use symbols designed to negate conventional adulthood. These symbols range from language to dress, personal adornment, and actual behavioral presentations of self.

The more an individual becomes involved in a subculture and the more radical the subculture, the more difficult it is for that person to come of age and enter mainstream adult society. Those who believe the latter world is oppressive would argue that this is not necessarily a bad thing. However, as we see in chapter 3, social dislocation can adversely affect the individual's identity formation and therefore his or her emotional well-being.

The subculture perspective on youth clearly advances our understanding of the problems some young people face. However, the majority of them do not become seriously involved in marginalized groups. Moreover, this perspective does not give us concrete clues as to how to rectify the deficient coming-of-age experiences that lead young people to turn to subcultures in the first place.

## Postmodern Views: Institutional Regulation

Postmodernism has been the subject of much recent debate.[45] In fact, the term *postmodern* is difficult to define, partly because it has been applied to so many different disciplines, ranging from art and architecture to the social sciences.[46] We will not attempt a definition here, except to say that the term is based on the premise that we have moved out of the modern era, in which science, linear logic, and order prevail, into a postmodern era where these things are rejected. Academic postmodern formulations put an emphasis on the subjective — how things are experienced is more important than any objective reality that might exist. In fact, the notion of an objective reality is problematized and to some extent rejected as unknowable.

There is not really an agreed-upon postmodern view of youth. Rather, this is an emerging, inchoate perspective. Nevertheless, we will present three accounts that place youth in a postmodern context. These can by no means be said to exhaust postmodern thinking on the matter, partly because that would be oxymoronic.

Richard Tinning and Lindsay Fitzclarence argue that a postmodern youth culture is emerging, not as a result of the actions of marginalized youths, as the subculture view would have it, but because of the impact of modern information technologies spread by global capitalism.[47] In effect, these technologies are part of a new transglobal institution made possible by the mass media. Following Henry Giroux,[48] they argue that these technologies create a sense of alienation among youth, because of their emphasis on individualism, and they are a source of boredom because it is difficult for mainstream activities like schooling to compete. While institutions like the family, education, and the workplace continue to be important in the socialization of the young, Tinning and Fitzclarence argue that

> in postmodernity, the media plays a primary role as a mediator for each of these social organizations. Adolescents' very perceptions of, and experiences within, each are shaped to a greater or lesser extent by experiences with information technology such as television, telephone, FM radio, video, and computer . . . postmodern adolescent life in Geelong, Australia, is increasingly linked to life in Los Angeles, Tokyo, and Berlin.[49]

Rather than taking a negative view of these influences, the authors argue that they empower the young in the sense that they make it easier for them to be "producers of their own biographies."[50] As consumers of images and commodities, they can accept or reject these things depending on whether or not they suit "their life projects" of "self-making." Tinning and Fitzclarence warn that by not responding to these postmodern influences, modernist institutions like schools will suffer.

A second postmodern view of youth is offered by Gordon Tait.[51] Tait reiterates the belief that youth is a "cultural invention," but does so by linking the concept of youth to the "governmental formation of a specific type of self."[52] That is, he sees the period we call youth as a creation of state policies that have as their premise the notion that each individual must construct an adult self. Each person must do "work on the self," and on "self-government."[53] Following Michel Foucault[54] and Pierre Bourdieu,[55] he argues that through various institutional programs the state regulates how young people spend their time. These programs classify young people according to a grid of norms that identify who is abnormal, who is to be successful, and so forth. State activities provide a "habitus" for youth, a pattern of conduct associated with "a matrix of perceptions, appreciations, and actions."[56]

A third postmodernist view of youth can be described as a feminist one. This perspective also focuses on the regulation of the young, but emphasizes gender differences in this regulation. Mica Nava argues that young men and women do not "occupy public spheres to the same extent."[57] Young women are much more regulated in the home than are young men. In fact, Nava argues that the home is the "*principal* site and source for the operation of control" of young women (emphasis in original). This regulation often centers on their sexuality, which is also controlled in schools and within peer groups. Within peer groups, Nava argues, young males participate in this regulation "through reference to a notion of femininity which incorporates particular modes of sexual behaviour, deference and compliance."

Although Nava refers specifically to Great Britain in her formulations, she charges that the study of youth has been biased in its assumption that males and females can be understood with the same conceptualizations:

The differential regulation of boys and girls inside and out-side the family . . . is one of a range of phenomena which point to the inadequacy of the conceptualization of youth as a unitary category. . . . In these studies girls are simply unproblematically subsumed under the general category that defines one group of people to another, that is to say youth to adults. This approach obscures differences within the category. Emphasis on youth as a period situated between childhood and adulthood has resulted in the neglect of gender as a *relational* concept — of power rela-tions *between* boys and girls. [emphasis in original]

This author goes on to argue that gender "often structures the experience of youth quite as significantly as class does," and that "there are systematic differences which exist between the ways in which most males and females experience genera-tional boundaries and the process of becoming adult." Howev-er, she goes on to admit that "this is a largely unsubstantiated claim" given the lack of research into the matter.

While they are clearly relevant to conditions of advanced industrial societies, it is unclear to us how much these post-modern views advance the sociological understanding of youth, as opposed to simply restating it with different termi-nology. In some ways, the fundamental assumptions of post-modern views combine elements of older sociological models like the global village, media indoctrination, consumerism, alienation, instrumental versus expressive gender roles, and the fragmentation of self. In other ways, these views have a strong but contradictory ideological bent: for example, claim-ing to have uncovered the relativity of knowledge in an absolute manner; declaring the sovereignty of subjectivity over objectivity through resource to (implicit) objective prin-ciples; or claiming to undermine relative truths with their own absolute, but never articulated, truths.[58] It is also unclear how comprehensive the accounts are, particularly when the studies of youth have focused on single institutions like the media, the state, the family, or peer groups. Moreover, the role played by capitalism in coming-of-age processes is underanalyzed or ignored. Nava's charge regarding the gender bias in theories of youth appears to have substance but this is not a new point,[59] and it is easy to overestimate its importance. This is also the case with her unsubstantiated charge that gender is a more significant concept than class in understanding youth experiences. Having explored the possible relevance of specific institutional regulation of youth, we turn to the political economy view, which predates the postmodern perspective.

## Political Economy Views: The State and Capital

As with the postmodern view of youth, the political economy one is not necessarily a widely circulated or agreed-upon perspective, but it does provide insights not forthcoming from other analyses. From this perspective, what is important is not how youth react, but rather what caused their reaction in the first place. Thus, this perspective goes beyond the previous sociological perspectives while building on some of their descriptions of social organization. The search for the cause of youth reactions begins with objective conditions produced by the distribution of power, particularly economic and political power.[60] Young people are seen as constituting a class without power, which is disenfranchised economically, politically, and socially. However, in order to mask this disenfranchisement and to ensure that young people do not mobilize as a reaction against their exploitation, it has been necessary for the state to impose a long period of indoctrination into acquiescence and acceptance of existing power structures as normal, natural, good, and benign. The state does this in capitalist societies because it directly serves the interests of capital and those who control it. This indoctrination is accomplished mainly through the educational system, but other institutions such as the media also enter into complicity with it.

Sociologists who subscribe to this political economy perspective see many young people as having been conditioned into a state of false consciousness, in which they often accept and support arrangements that work directly against their own interests. In particular, these arrangements engender an alienation, especially from the essence of oneself as a self-determining, creative individual. Thus, young people so indoctrinated are taught to believe that society in general is benign; that the economy functions in the interest of the average person; that they will be duly rewarded if they work hard; that the educational system is based on merit; that they will get the jobs they want if they behave and work hard; and that they will live happily if they adopt a conventional life-style. Led to believe these things, they also accept that if something bad happens to them or to one of their peers, they are at fault, not the system. Thus, they are taught that their alienation is normal, and that they are responsible for any regrets they have about their lives. From a functionalist perspective, such attitudes indicate that the young person is well socialized; from this political economy perspective, however, the young person exhibits false consciousness and alienation.

Those who resent such control and manipulation are usually subjected to additional pressures that compensate for their supposedly inadequate socialization and convince them to accept their condition without blaming the system. These additional "cooling-out" pressures come from counselors, the police, the courts, social workers, psychologists, and teachers, all of whom are directly or indirectly paid by the state, and all of whom believe in what they are doing.[61] These pressures exist both inside and outside the educational system, and from the political economy perspective constitute an effective social control mechanism that quashes an oppressed group and protects the interests of the dominant economic interests and all of its beneficiaries.

Young people are also controlled financially, with limited access to other than the most exploitative jobs. Consequently, it is not difficult to control them emotionally, and to define their sense of self and their tastes. Thus, much of mainstream youth culture constitutes a special type of consumer culture. Young people are hungry to have their emotions, identity, and tastes defined and redefined for them by the massive industries that market fashion, music, art, and other consumer items. These goods all have in common an identity-conferring quality. To be "someone," to be "in," one has to have or consume a particular item. Young consumers are the perfect target for such manipulation because the fact that they have been marginalized from adult society and sequestered into groups at school based on grade levels makes them hunger for an identity. Because young people's identity is so precarious, the industries we have mentioned can make their products obsolete or constantly change them year after year, requiring consumers to follow the trends they arbitrarily set and announce through the media. From this political economy perspective, the entire capitalist system works in unison and is the perfect arrangement for enterprises that have as their primary objective profit maximization regardless of the social costs.

While the political economy perspective appears to round out the other sociological views by specifying *why* the social order is the way it is and *how* it changes, like the other sociological views it is primarily macro in orientation. As such it does not provide the concepts by which we can understand things like the psychology of false consciousness and the micro manipulation of identities. In chapter 3, we introduce a theory that does so. In part 2, we more fully develop the political economy view.

## Problems with Nurture Approaches

The nurture perspectives clearly add much to our understanding of the social environment confronting the young as they come of age. Some criticize sociological views, which range from the conservatism of functionalism to the radicalism of the political economy perspective, for being too politicized. However, as we saw with the nature approaches, the same charge can be made of any perspective — all are embedded in assumptions posed either for or against vested interests. In this book we are trying to present a *comprehensive* explanation of coming of age in advanced industrial society.

Further, we believe perspectives should be judged on the evidence, and not by whether they correspond with one's personal political viewpoint or professional interests. In the next chapter, we examine a variety of statistical evidence that helps us assess the usefulness of the perspectives discussed above.

Sociological perspectives have also been criticized because they tend to reduce all behavior to social structural causes.[62] While there is some truth to this charge, sociologists have attempted to address this problem, as evidenced by the so-called agency-structure debate. As we saw, both the postmodern and the political economy views of the coming-of-age process attempt to deal with this problem, but as we illustrate in chapter 3 an additional conceptual framework is necessary to explain fully the human capacity for agency, that is, the capacity for acting intentionally and willfully in the social world.

Finally, it is easy to ignore the fact that humans are animals with certain inherent characteristics and capacities, however subtle they might be. We are creatures whose essence is rooted in biology; the question is just how important these biological roots are. Thus, what follows is an approach that tries to accommodate biology into a model of human behavior as it is relevant to coming-of-age processes.

## A SPECULATIVE INTERDISCIPLINARY APPROACH

Having argued that biology has at best an indirect effect on the phenomenon of adolescence, let us speculate on the possibility that a fundamental incongruity exists between the conditions imposed on young people in advanced industrial societies and their actual needs. One way to do this is to think of the human animal and its similarity to other species. When we look at other species and their instinctual reactions to puberty, interesting points of comparison emerge. We make these cross-species comparisons for heuristic purposes only, in that they provide a model that specifies points of interaction between nature and nurture as humans mature into adulthood.[63]

Lawrence Steinberg argues from an evolutionary perspective that if animals do not leave the nest or family at the time of puberty or shortly thereafter, they are literally evicted.[64] This is the case among our closest evolutionary relatives, the primates, who are subjected to the wrath of the parent(s) if they do not leave the family following puberty. It is interesting to look at what happens to primates living in captivity where a departure of the young is impeded. Among many species in captivity, puberty is actually delayed while the offspring remains with the parents. Among tamarinds and marmosets, for example, female pubertal development is inhibited by the presence of the mother. When the mother is taken away, puberty can begin within days. Steinberg suggests that this constitutes an evolutionary adaptation, whereby genetic diversity is increased because the possibility of inbreeding is minimized. He further argues that interpersonal conflict between parents and their pubescent offspring may have an evolutionary basis, ensuring that postpubertal offspring are dispersed.

Steinberg contends that offspring in Western cultures left the parental home shortly after puberty until only quite recently. Citing historical evidence, he notes that individuals often did not live with their parents beyond puberty until the last century. Before industrialization, Western culture practiced *extrusion*, namely, the placing of individuals out of the home at, or following, puberty. This often involved a period of semiautonomy, during which the young person worked productively but was still accountable to an adult authority. Contact with the parents was not normally lost, but excessive contact that might give rise to irrational conflicts was avoided. Hence, the young were enfranchised as adults in a steadily increasing manner. Baumeister and Tice describe a similar phenomenon in the United States, noting that before "1800, the status of teenagers is best characterized as 'semidependent.' Although legally they had few autonomous rights, in daily life they were neither supported nor supervised by their parents."[65]

In a similar vein, in many cultures, the pubertal rite of passage was associated with the process of separation from parents, following which the young person assumed some degree of autonomy and new responsibility. Today, however, vestiges of these rites, such as confirmations and bar mitzvahs, are seen more as social events than as a formal ceremony designed to mark impending adulthood. Indeed, young people now have a long way to go before this kind of recognition will be granted them. In this light, coming of age in advanced industrial societies involves a number of minor and sometimes insignificant rites of passage, which actually do not confer many meaningful *rights*.

As mentioned previously, it appears that industrialization has had the effect of forcing young people to remain wholly dependent upon their parents and to endure the many conflicts that often result from forced cohabitation. In these conflicts parents generally prevail, because they have the greater economic, social, and legal power. While such an imbalance of power can be seen as reasonable under many circumstances, when parents do not use their authority judiciously, their offspring inevitably suffer. One cannot always assume that parents behave rationally when faced with some conflicts, especially if we accept the fact that some of this tension is based on an inherent incompatability between them and their offspring attempting to come of age. Thus, we can speculate that we are jeopardizing the ability of our culture to adapt to new challenges through the unfair treatment many young people are subjected to under the current prolongation of youth.

As we also noted previously, industrial societies have produced conditions under which many individuals experience puberty four years earlier than they did in the last century, primarily because of improved nutrition and health standards. These sexually mature individuals must now postpone assuming full adult work and family roles for at least a decade and often two decades. If we allow Steinberg's argument, during this prolonged adolescence most are financially and emotionally dependent upon their parents, who appear to have traces of an inherent antagonism toward them. With extended education, many young people also find themselves under the charge of other adult authorities.

There is also an inherent antagonism in these relations because these parental surrogates have the formally sanctioned authority to shape and "correct" those who cannot or do not want to conform to the conditions imposed by this new stage of life. Many young people find themselves struggling against these constraints in order to discover and establish an identity.

Indeed, the sociologists who subscribe to the political economy view remind us that in contemporary Western societies, the young are now legally denied the opportunity to come of age in some ways, as in the case of labor-force participation. When they are finally permitted to join the work force, they are often exploited: they get the lowest paying jobs, often on a part-time basis with no benefits. This, of course, benefits the employer, not the young person. In this way young people are marginalized in the labor force and also excluded from mainstream adult society and therefore from sources of power.[66] Without economic, social, and political representation, they have fewer rights, privileges, and status. While this trend began with the child protection movement, the process of exclusion continued to cover those in their early teen years de jure, and it now affects de facto some who are well into their late 20s, namely, those competing for post-secondary educational credentials.

We believe that an interdisciplinary view is necessary to take us beyond limited singular perspectives. Coming of age in advanced industrial societies is a complex phenomenon that requires a multifaceted approach. The speculative view makes way for a notion of intentionality, or agency, as a facet of the young person, as opposed to him or her being totally determined by external factors (whether the factors be social rewards and punishments or social institutions). As individuals with inherent needs and the capacity to come of age in their own right, the young can be seen as acting intentionally to find meaning in their lives, a process that involves willfully choosing between alternative courses of action and consciously resisting oppressive conditions.

Finally, as with most theories, all of the perspectives examined in this chapter are valid to the extent that each contains an element of truth that can be empirically verified. In terms of understanding social change and the position of the young in advanced industrial society, it is most useful to employ those perspectives that best help us understand how coming of age has changed from preindustrial, through industrial, to advanced industrial society, as well as ones that help us to understand how the newly structured coming-of-age processes are experienced by different young people. Thus, we will rely on the sociological perspectives discussed so far and will look particularly to the political economy model for a comprehensive overview of this change. After all, advanced industrial societies in the West are all capitalist, so we should look at the role played by capitalism in shaping coming-of-age processes.

# 2

---

# The Liabilities of Youth in Advanced Industrial Society

---

Now that we have explored a number of theoretical perspectives concerning adolescence and youth we can examine shifts in the institutional and economic structures of advanced industrial society that are affecting the fortunes of the young. Our examination of contemporary youth is based on empirical evidence drawn largely from Canada and the United States. Clearly, parallels between these countries exist, given their closely linked economies. The two nations differ mainly in terms of the extent of their social safety nets, with Canada having the more extensive one.

We suspect that many of the trends affecting young people in the United States and Canada can be found in other Western industrial societies. Because a larger cross-cultural study has not yet been undertaken, we recognize the risks of generalizing. On the other hand, our supposition is based on the fact that Western countries have similar economic structures and state policies affecting youth. Certainly, readers will concede that economic and cultural globalization processes are resulting in the homogenization of life-styles, even outside Western countries.

If we were to generalize about the coming of age process in other Western nations, undoubtedly serious divergences and exceptions would be found. For example, youth unemployment in Britain, apprenticeships in Germany, and educational attainment in Japan are phenomena unique to each of those countries.[1] In spite of specific divergences, we believe that many of the processes we see in Canada and the United States apply to other advanced industrial nations. When there are slightly different economic trends and social policies in a particular nation, somewhat different circumstances will be thrust upon the young people of that nation. However, we feel that coming-of-age patterns are similar in Western countries and that national differences are of degree rather than of kind. This assumption also applies within countries with regard to differences arising from race, gender, and class. It would be fruitful for other researchers to investigate these trends in other Western countries.

Issues arising from differences in gender,[2] race, class, and nationality certainly color young people's life experiences.[3] But they do have their youth in common, and it is this shared characteristic that often affects how the adult community treats them. As we have seen, certain formal structures are in place that allow adults to regulate the young and exclude them from their society. Advanced industrial society has introduced or modified several such structures of regulation and exclusion.

## CREDENTIALISM AND EDUCATION INFLATION

Jeffrey Mirel notes that in the first quarter of the present century, few Americans in their mid-teens were still in school. Instead, most entered the workforce, assuming adult independence and contributing to their family's income. For example, in urban areas, young women entered the labor force in increasing numbers, "particularly in office and factory work. Young men helped their fathers in the fields, apprenticed in crafts and trades, or worked in the expanding manufacturing and service industries."[4] At that

**Table 2.1**

## High-school and college enrollments in the United States over the past century*

| Percentage of young people aged 14 to 17 attending school:** | Percentage of young people aged 18 to 21 attending college:*** |
|---|---|
| 1890 — 6 | 1880 — 2 |
| 1900 — 10 | 1890 — 3 |
| 1910 — 16 | 1900 — 4 |
| 1920 — 30 | 1920 — 8 |
| 1930 — 50 | 1940 — 16 |
| 1940 — 70 | 1950 — 30 |
| 1950 — 75 | 1970 — 48 |
| 1960 — 85 | |
| 1970 — 90 | |
| 1980 — 90 | |

*All figures adapted from Schultze et al. 1991
**Adapted by Schultze et al. from Elder (1987)
***Adapted by Schultze et al. from Lefkowitz-Horowitz (1987)

time, it was still widely believed that "early entry of young people into the working world was both economically and educationally vital." Table 2.1 shows how school enrollment in the United States has dramatically increased during the past century. Today, the norm is to stay in high school, and not to do so is considered unacceptable.

This norm means that those coming of age now face the prospect of remaining in school for a prolonged period primarily in order to attain high levels of educational credentials. While this may seem like a trite observation, at the core of this phenomenon called "credentialism" is the assumption that the best way to prepare oneself for a job is through formal educational training. Yet, as has been argued elsewhere,[5] for most jobs the amount of academic training currently required is either unnecessary or irrelevant. In fact, it appears that the required level of credentials is often based on the needs of the monopolistic educational system and the desire of certain occupational groups to acquire more status and wealth instead of on actual demands in the workplace. Many younger people are competing to do the same work as their parents, but they are only allowed to do it if they have attained a higher level of education. Thus, those coming of age must deal with "education inflation" — an inflationary spiral in the number of credentials it takes to secure a good job.

As a consequence of education inflation, numerous jobs that once required only a high-school education now require a university education, despite the fact that many of the jobs are essentially the same. This is especially true of sales, service, and clerical jobs. Even without consulting statistics, one can see that the level of skills needed for many of these positions has not changed appreciably in several decades, and that the qualifications requirement is therefore unjustified. But to use the statistics, American research indicates that about two-thirds of all jobs are so simple that they require only a few weeks of on-the-job training.[6] In addition, Ivor Berg has argued that only about 15 percent of jobs in the United States between 1940 and 1960 underwent a skill upgrading, while the remaining 85 percent involved workers doing the same things but with a higher level of education.[7] Canadian research indicates that in 1981, about 66 percent of all jobs in the labor force required less than 12 months "specific vocational training" (compared to 72 percent in 1961). When the workers themselves are asked, the training period becomes even shorter: 44 percent say that their jobs can be learned in less than a month.[8]

Furthermore, many of the newer jobs involving the much-revered computer require only a couple of weeks training for someone with grade nine reading and arithmetic levels, because most only involve inputting data.[9] Indeed, a major consequence of modern technology is the deskilling of segments of the labor force, which makes certain jobs routine, boring, and unimaginative.[10] The checkout counter in a supermarket provides a readily observable case. Computers now read the prices of products and the clerk merely has to pass a label over a scanner. If that does not work, a product code is punched in, and if that fails someone with computer skills is called for help. Virtually no arithmetic or computer skills are needed for one of the most common clerical jobs![11]

We are not arguing that a significant portion of jobs do not require highly skilled workers. We are challenging the persistent belief that more and more education is required of *all* the population for the economy to be viable and for individuals to be fully competent in the modern workplace. This belief is partly responsible for the fact that in Canada, between 1950 and 1990, the number of full-time postsecondary students increased ninefold.[12] During the 1980s alone, enrollment in many Canadian postsecondary institutions jumped by 50 percent. Now, over one million people are attending Canadian postsecondary institutions out of a population of some 27 million.

While there are numerous possible benefits to higher education, many young people suffer because they believe that they must have postsecondary credentials to find jobs or because they have no choice but to get the credentials to compete for jobs which, in fact, do not require specific skills related to their degrees. This problem becomes very apparent when we examine the linkage between higher education and the workplace in relation to the problem of underemployment, a widespread phenomenon that is unique to advanced industrial societies.

We can examine the tenuous nature of this linkage in the context of underemployment by looking at a series of national surveys carried out in Canada. For example, the Class of 1976 university graduates was surveyed in 1978 and the following statistics were compiled: one-third reported being in clerical, sales, or other low-paying jobs; 40 percent with social science degrees said they were in jobs having nothing to do with their field of study; and one-third explicitly said that they were underemployed.[13]

More recent figures indicate that the situation worsened in the 1980s. From a nationwide study in Canada of the Class of 1982, anywhere from 20 percent of those in the natural sciences to more than 50 percent of those in the social sciences found themselves underemployed two years after graduation, that is, they were forced to work in jobs that explicitly did not require a university degree.[14] A five-year follow-up of the Class of '82 found that 35 percent of those employed were still in jobs that did not require a university degree (ranging from 24 percent in engineering and applied science to 40 percent in the social sciences and 45 percent in general arts and sciences). Moreover, only 49 percent of social science graduates revealed that they held jobs that were "directly related to their education."[15]

As chart 2.1 shows, the Canadian Class of '86 had much the same experience as their predecessors: 41 percent of those holding undergraduate degrees were working in jobs that "did not require university level qualifications."[16] Even more shocking is the finding that those with master's degrees experienced even higher levels of underemployment. Two years after graduating, 62 percent of M.A. holders from the Class of '86 were working in jobs that did not require university-level qualifications. Five years after graduation, 57 percent of master's graduates from the Class of '82 were similarly underemployed. Furthermore, for those with Ph.D.s, these figures were 35 percent and 40 percent respectively.

A similar problem of underemployment has emerged in the United States over the past 20 years. Between 1968 and 1978, 25 percent of college graduates accepted jobs that were previously held by less educated workers.[17] While the underemployment estimate was about 10 percent in the late 1960s, it rose steadily during the 1970s, doubling by the 1980s to just below 20 percent, where it has held relatively steady.[18] A more recent estimate puts the overall underemployment figure at 17.5 percent,[19] but none of these estimates is based on a nationwide graduating class from a given year, which would likely give a higher estimate.[20] Indeed, according to Daniel Hecker estimates for the Classes of 1984 and 1986 indicate that "almost 40 percent of the graduates awarded bachelor's degrees . . . reported *that they thought* a degree was not needed to obtain the job they held a year after graduation."[21]

What emerges from this analysis of the changing educational system of advanced industrial society is that credentialism is exerting a normative pressure on the coming-of-age process — it is leading to an increasing pro-

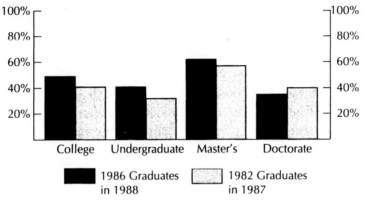

**Chart 2.1**

**Proportions of recent Canadian college and university graduates who are underemployed by level of qualification, 1987 and 1988**

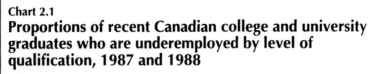

| | 1986 Graduates in 1988 | 1982 Graduates in 1987 |

Note that about one-half of community college graduates were underemployed two years after graduating in 1986. The situation was marginally improved for 1982 graduates five years after graduation in 1987. The circumstances were somewhat better for university undergraduates, but worse for those with master's degrees. Those with doctorates faced a slightly better situation, but about one-third were still underemployed two years after graduation and 40 percent were in this predicament five years after graduation.

From: Nobert, McDowell, and Goulet, 1992.

longation of youth. At the same time, despite the scramble for credentials, it is obvious that the advanced industrial economy does not need as many university graduates as the educational system is putting out. Thus, there is a "normative cross-pressure" on those coming of age,[22] which is disenfrachising many of them and causing them to lose faith in the belief that education is the way to success. As we have seen, in spite of holding one or more degrees, many find themselves in unskilled jobs, where they are forced to work for the lowest wages and minimal benefits because they lost the credentialism game. Many of those who end up winning the game have a head start in terms of their class background, race, and gender.

## "COOLING OUT THE MARK"

The above analysis points to a situation in which there is a serious disjuncture between educational experiences and first contact with adulthood for many young people. It would appear that the belief regarding the role of education in job training is part of a self-fulfilling prophecy, which often has little to do with the reality of the workplace. For example, if many people believe that a great deal of training is necessary to perform a certain job, that training will become a requirement, and therefore everyone doing the job will acquire those skills, regardless of whether they actually use them.

John Porter has argued that the university degree is becoming associated with a bimodal distribution in terms of job privilege, with "the highly qualified at one end and the mass of less qualified [with no degrees] at the other."[23] In Canada, this problem may be particularly severe, given that it has both a moderate drop-out rate from high school *and* a high university attendance rate in relation to other Organization for Economic Cooperation and Development (OECD) countries.[24] As we see below, John Myles and associates have identified a concomitant "declining middle" in the occupational structure that is specifically affecting young people.[25] Even so, a university degree has become a necessary but not sufficient requirement for entry into privileged positions. Thus, the university degree is increasingly sought after as just one more form of capital,[26] regulated by credentialing educational institutions. Now the degree is a passport that allows one to travel the road to success, but it certainly is not a ticket to success.

For those who have no hope of even acquiring this passport, the system of credentialism plays a cruel trick. As Reginald Bibby and Donald Posterski argue, we "extol the virtues of a university degree and relegate everything else to second-class status. Young people set their sights accordingly."[27] They go on to note that while over 50 percent of the 15- to 19-year-old group expect to get such a degree in Canada, only 15 percent of the age cohort will actually register in university.[28]

Thus, they charge that we "are guilty of cultural overpromising. Young people are being duped. . . . The harsh reality is that before most young people turn 20 they have to deal with the disillusionment of their educational dreams." The words of a recent Ontario government youth commissioner echo this assertion. He was shocked to discover that:

> Excluding private schools, 40% of students in Ontario beginning in grade 9 do not graduate from grade 12; 76% do not graduate from grade 13; only 31% go on to college or university; only about two-thirds of them graduate. Put another way, for a medium-sized Ontario city with 10 high schools, the equivalent of *one* school of grade 12 bound students, and one-and-one half schools of grade 13 bound students disappears *each year.*[29]

More recently, Andy Hargreaves and Ivor Goodson showed how the drop-out rate fluctuates according to the type of program a student is enrolled in: "In Ontario, in 1988, general level programs accounted for 72% of dropouts, basic level programs for 18 percent and advanced level programs for 10 percent."[30] It seems that only about one-half of high-school dropouts in Canada eventually return to school.[31] This would mean that the high-school completion rate should present a different picture. Even so, the most recent picture indicates that 21 percent of those aged 18 to 20 who were no longer attending high school in 1991 had not graduated.[32] Thus, the noncompletion estimate is 24 percent for males and 16 percent for females.[33]

Chart 2.2 provides some international comparisons of the drop-out rate among 17-year-olds, indicating that Canada has among the highest percentage of the advanced industrial nations, while the United States is somewhere in the middle.[34] Chart 2.3 shows the drop-out rate for the United States in 1989, broken down by race and ethnicity. Note that the rate for Hispanics is high, whereas for blacks it is close to the national average.[35]

Even students who actually make it through high school and on to university still have a difficult road to travel, because many are weeded out during these studies. In the

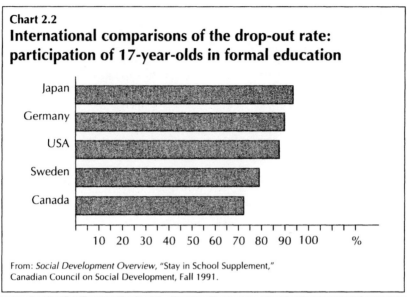

**Chart 2.2**

**International comparisons of the drop-out rate: participation of 17-year-olds in formal education**

|  | |
|---|---|
| Japan | |
| Germany | |
| USA | |
| Sweden | |
| Canada | |

10  20  30  40  50  60  70  80  90  100    %

From: *Social Development Overview*, "Stay in School Supplement," Canadian Council on Social Development, Fall 1991.

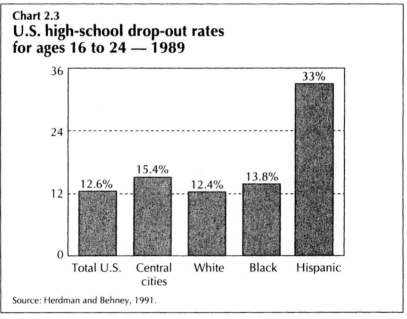

**Chart 2.3**

**U.S. high-school drop-out rates for ages 16 to 24 — 1989**

| | 12.6% | 15.4% | 12.4% | 13.8% | 33% |
|---|---|---|---|---|---|
| | Total U.S. | Central cities | White | Black | Hispanic |

Source: Herdman and Behney, 1991.

United States, only 50 percent of those who register in undergraduate programs graduate within five years.[36] In Canada, this figure is about 58 percent and appears to be decreasing; even when the period between registration and graduation is extended to 13 years, the degree completion rate is only about 72 percent.[37] However, considerable variation exists between universities (the range of incompletion is from 15 percent to 68 percent, and is affected by how selective the institution is in accepting new students). The incompletion rate is very high among part-time students (it ranges from 63 percent to 89 percent), and women have lower incompletion rates than men.[38]

Those who are weeded out or "cooled out" of the educational system and must therefore travel the occupational journey without the requisite credentials face considerable financial difficulties. Chart 2.4 illustrates the lifelong implications of having less than a full high-school education in Canada. Note that women are particularly disadvantaged, regardless of whether they finish high school. Chart 2.5 shows how race and ethnicity interact with unemployment among dropouts in the United States. Almost one-half of black dropouts were unemployed in 1986 compared with about one-fifth of white dropouts.

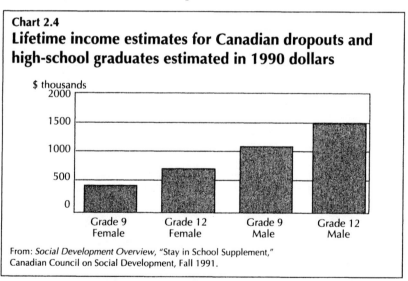

**Chart 2.4**
**Lifetime income estimates for Canadian dropouts and high-school graduates estimated in 1990 dollars**

From: *Social Development Overview,* "Stay in School Supplement," Canadian Council on Social Development, Fall 1991.

In Canada, one-third of the population is involved in the educational system, either as students, teachers, or administrators.[39] Education is big business. However, businesses

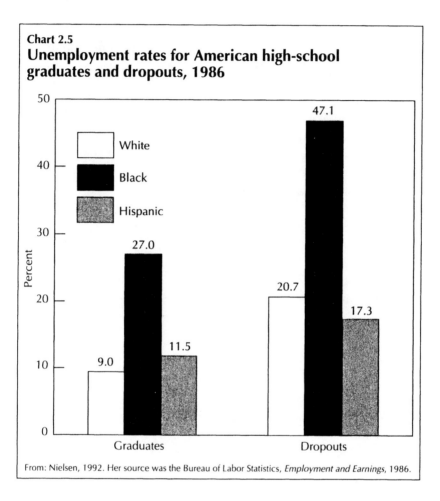

**Chart 2.5**
**Unemployment rates for American high-school graduates and dropouts, 1986**

Legend:
- White
- Black
- Hispanic

Graduates:
- White: 9.0
- Black: 27.0
- Hispanic: 11.5

Dropouts:
- White: 20.7
- Black: 47.1
- Hispanic: 17.3

Y-axis: Percent (0 to 50)

From: Nielsen, 1992. Her source was the Bureau of Labor Statistics, *Employment and Earnings*, 1986.

normally seek to satisfy their customers. How is it, then, that the education business gets away with not giving so many "customers" full value for their money? What is this monolithic system doing to young people and to society at large? But most important, why are so many people, both young and old, unaware of what is taking place? We believe that the answer to some of these questions comes with the realization that the educational system is in many ways a holdover from the industrial era and is still "defined for the age of large factories and heavy industry. . . . [While] the surface and style of schooling may have changed . . . the industrial period has inscribed the parameters and possibilities with which . . . contemporary . . . schools operate."[40]

What we have seen is evidence of an educational monopoly that rose to its ascendency during the industrial period, but which is now out of control. The vision that unlimited education would result in unlimited economic growth simply has not been realized. Instead, we see an inflationary spiral of credentials that has set in motion a scramble for credentials as part of a gamble for success. We are now at the point where virtually all young people must get in the game because the ante has been raised for everyone.[41] But as with poker, there are many more losers than winners.

## THE NEW SERVICE WORKER

Both the winners and the losers in the credentialing game face different experiences than did their parents when they came of age. Chart 2.6 provides us with a long-term view of

---

**Chart 2.6**
### The changing distribution of major occupational groups in Canada, 1911–1986

| Category | 1911 | 1931 | 1951 | 1971 | 1986 |
|---|---|---|---|---|---|
| Service | 9% | 10% | 11% | 12% | 14% |
| Commercial/financial | 6% | 7% | 8% | 11% | 10% |
| Manufacturing/mechanical | 16% | 13% | 18% | 20% | 16% |
| Other* | 23% | 24% | 28% | 19% | 21% |
| Professional | 4% | 7% | 8% | 14% | 16% |
| Clerical | 4% | 8% | 12% | 18% | 19% |
| Agriculture | 38% | 32% | 17% | 7% | 4% |

*Managerial, transportation, construction, forestry, fishing, and mining occupations.

From: O'Neill, 1991.

---

the way the occupational structure has changed in Canada from 1911 to 1986. The most striking thing is the decline in the agricultural sector. The latter represented 38 percent of all occupations in 1911 but only 4 percent in 1986. Moreover, in the 10-year period between 1979 and 1989, "service industry employment grew by 29 percent [such that] . . . in 1989, 70 percent of all workers were in service industries . . . up from 65 percent in 1979."[42] No longer are there large numbers of young people coming of age on the farm, whose first work experience is in agricultural labor. Instead, most must now fit into one of the expanding service industries. Of particular interest in this chart is the fact that in Canada the size of the manufacturing sector has not changed significantly during this century. In fact, in 1986 it was the same size as in 1911, when it represented 16 percent of the labor force. This is one reason why we use the term *advanced industrial* instead of *postindustrial*. What has changed is that agricultural jobs have been replaced by service, clerical, and professional jobs.

Jeff O'Neill has examined the age trends behind shifts in the Canadian occupational structure:

> Perhaps the most important shift in occupations that cannot be explained in large part by demographic trends, occurred among young adults. In 1986, the representation of people aged 15–24 was highest in service occupations (34%), while in 1951 the highest proportion of this age group was in clerical occupations (40%). This was largely due to the proportion of service occupations filled by people in this age group, which increased from 27% in 1951. In contrast, the proportion of clerical occupations filled by those aged 15–24 declined to 26% in 1986.[43]

Another study confirms the fact that young people are increasingly found in service jobs instead of clerical ones.[44] We have already seen that service jobs are becoming deskilled, less well paid, and thus more likely to be subordinate positions. Hence, young people are becoming more ghettoized in the service industries, along with other disadvantaged groups. Gary Fine, Jeylan Mortimer, and Donald

Roberts lay out in stark detail how things have also changed for young Americans and how these changes have been masked by various myths:

> The positive rhetoric surrounding the employment of young people appears to be predicated on the image of the apprentice actively learning a craft or skill under the guidance of a more experienced master. In previous eras young people worked on the farm, in factories, and in the crafts in positions that led to adult careers, but today teenagers work primarily in the retail and service sectors in positions earmarked for youth or for other transient workers. These positions provide little opportunity for advancement or for exercising authority, and the pay is low. . . . Tasks are often simple and repetitive (stocking shelves, cleaning, carrying), and therefore require little training, special skill, or knowledge acquired in school. . . . The youth workplace, furthermore, is highly age segregated, offering little opportunity to emulate, or even have contact with, responsible adults.[45]

John Myles, G. Picot, and Ted Wannell examined changes in the Canadian workplace during the early 1980s and concluded that they reflect a "declining middle" in the sense that there is an increasing concentration of jobs in the bottom and the upper-middle segments of the wage distribution. They account for this in terms of changes in the structure of employment, mainly a growth in jobs in the service industries. Their principal conclusion was that while occupational restructuring was having an effect on the declining middle and producing a decline in relative wages, "the primary change in all sectors of the economy, was a decline in the relative wage rates of young people . . . [and] an increase in the relative wage rates of middle-aged workers."[46] In other words, the declining middle is primarily an age-based phenomenon.

It is important to emphasize that Myles and his colleagues also concluded that this major shift was not due to a generational or recession effect; rather it occurred "in all industrial sectors, occupational groups, regions and all levels of education."[47] Moreover, the increasing prevalence of part-time work accounted for little of this change. They also observed a similar pattern in the United States and in European economies. In short, young workers lost earning power regardless of the sector of the economy in which they worked, so even those who managed to avoid service jobs were still vulnerable to this shift. With the declining middle, it is also likely that the prospects for advancement of many young people will diminish. In contrast, for "older workers, the 'declining middle' . . . had largely meant movement into jobs with higher wage rates. . . . Middle aged and older workers seem to have consolidated their middle class standing."[48]

Clearly, young people are the biggest losers as the conditions of advanced industrial society have become entrenched. The contradiction between credentialism and occupational disenfranchisement[49] sends many of those attempting to come of age on an extended journey that does not lead them to the independence of adulthood, but rather to the uncertainties of prolonged youth. Let us now examine the toll this is taking on them.

## STATISTICAL INDICATORS OF CHANGE

We continue our examination of coming of age in advanced industrial society by examining in detail a number of statistical indicators that show what life is like for those trying to make their way to adulthood, especially in the face of education inflation and declining job prospects. When we review these indicators, a picture emerges of a deterioration in quality of life and opportunities, particularly since the 1950s, when the current occupational structure began to take shape. (It was during this period that the number of agricultural jobs declined and service jobs increased.) We find, for example, increases in unemployment and poverty and relative decreases in wages, as well as increases in the suicide rate and various types of psychological and physical maladies. We believe that many of these problems, which have burgeoned over the past few decades, are a result of changes in the way the young must come of age.

We have organized these statistics to reflect the perspective suggested in Mead's *Coming of Age in Samoa*, which assumes that the young should be welcomed and guided by adults as they enter this stage of life. In addition, readers should note that we are principally concerned with young people 15 years of age and over, not those in early adolescence who are still dealing with rapid physical development and the residual influences of modern childhood. We begin with statistics related to the former group's integration into the economy, and by implication, its movement toward adult roles.

## Socioeconomic Changes

*Earning Power.*   A feature of advanced industrial societies that is affecting the young is a redistribution of wealth, whereby older age groups (typically those between 35 and 65 years) are getting more of the national wealth. In Canada, for example, Ted Wannell notes that the "average real wage of workers aged 16–24 in 1986 was down almost $1.50 per hour, or 17%, from 1981" in 1986 inflation-adjusted dollars. However, adjusted "average wages for workers aged 35 and over were higher" during this period.[50] Wages for the 35- to 49-year-old group rose almost six percent, while those for the 50- to 64-year-old one rose eight percent. Wannell's figures are presented in chart 2.7. Even a cursory glance reveals an age-related trend in this chart. When we scrutinize these figures, this impression is confirmed. In fact, we find an almost perfect correlation between the four age groups and percentage of income change, suggesting a strong relationship between economic franchise and age.

In their analysis of the same set of data, Myles, Picot, and Wannell looked at gender differences in addition to age differences. They found that young women experienced basically the same decline in earning power as young men:

> In jobs held by women age 16–24, there was a net shift of almost 20 percent out of [higher] wage levels . . . into the very bottom wage category. By 1986, almost 60 percent of

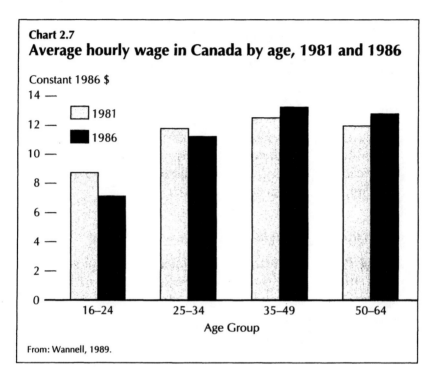

**Chart 2.7**
**Average hourly wage in Canada by age, 1981 and 1986**

Constant 1986 $

☐ 1981
■ 1986

Age Group

From: Wannell, 1989.

jobs held by young women were in the two lowest wage levels [of the workforce. Similarly, the] downward trend in wages in jobs held by young men was almost as large. There was a net shift of 18 percent out of the higher wage levels into [the two lowest wage levels]. These two bottom levels accounted for 44.2 percent of the jobs held by young males in 1986.[51]

Myles and his co-researchers also note that in the 35 to 49 age group both men and women experienced gains in earning power, while in the over 50 category only men experienced a gain.

The Canadian shift in earning power is replicated in American data. From the American statistics, however, we can gain a sense of how different ethnic and racial subgroupings of youth are being affected economically and we can see the trend over a longer period. Table 2.2 presents information regarding annual earnings for 20- to 24-year-olds bro-

**Table 2.2**

## Trends in the real mean annual earnings of 20- to 24-year-old American civilian males, 1973–1986, by educational attainment and race/ethnic group

**(in 1986 Dollars)**

| | All Males (20–24) | | % Change in Earnings 1973–1986 | | | |
| | | | | | African | |
| | 1973 | 1986 | All | White | American | Hispanic |
|---|---|---|---|---|---|---|
| All males | $12,166 | $9,027 | -25.8 | -21.0 | -46.0 | -29.0 |
| Males with less than high-school education | 11,815 | 6,853 | -42.0 | -42.3 | -60.6 | -27.3 |
| High-school graduates | 15,221 | 10,924 | -28.2 | -24.4 | 43.8 | -34.5 |
| Some college | 13,108 | 10,960 | -16.4 | -11.3 | -42.7 | -21.2 |
| College graduates | 14,630 | 13,759 | -6.0 | -5.6 | +6.5 | N.A. |

From: The William T. Grant Foundation Commission on Work, Family, and Citizenship, 1988.

ken down by race or ethnicity and class (as measured by educational attainment) in the United States. This table illustrates that between 1973 and 1986 the economic prospects for young American males declined on average by 26 percent, when measured in terms of earning power. White males experienced the least decline (21 percent), while African-American males experienced the most (46 percent). The lowest class of African Americans (having less than high-school education) experienced the most severe decline (61 percent), while the highest class of white males experienced the least severe decline (six percent). Numerous comparisons can be made in this table, but it is clear that the structure of economic privilege in advanced industrial America includes age, as well as race and class.

Chart 2.8 puts this disenfranchisement of American youth in a context similar to Canadian youth, as illustrated in chart 2.7. We see in chart 2.8 that young American men now make less than 70 percent of what older men make, whereas in 1967 near parity (about 94 percent) existed between the two groups. Clearly, then, the decline in earning power is at least partly specific to age and has occurred over the period we have been discussing.

***Independence from Parents.*** Given diminishing economic prospects, it is not surprising that more young people are continuing to live with their parents for longer periods of time — other alternatives are often not available. For instance, in Canada recent figures show that between 1981 and 1986 the percentage of unmarried young adults living with their parents increased steadily. Monica Boyd and Ed Pryor observe that this shift is most noticeable among unmarried people between the ages of 20 and 29: as of 1986, six out of 10 women between the ages of 20 to 24 were living with

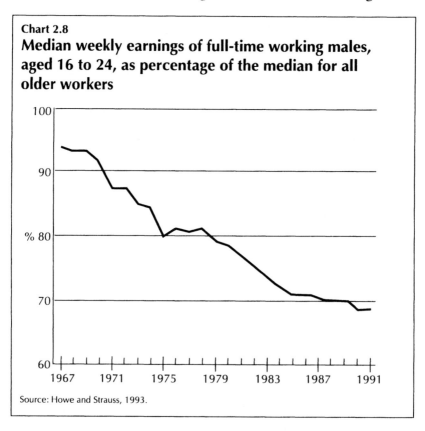

**Chart 2.8**
**Median weekly earnings of full-time working males, aged 16 to 24, as percentage of the median for all older workers**

Source: Howe and Strauss, 1993.

one or both parents, while the figure for men was seven out of 10. Among those in their late 20s, these figures are still quite high: "over four out of ten unattached or unmarried men and three out of ten women were living at home."[52] These authors speculate that contemporary "young adults . . . will spend more time in a homelife over which they exert less than full control, possibly in the process adopting their parents' behaviour patterns more thoroughly."[53] Even a university education does not guarantee independent living arrangements: according to Harvey Krahn and Graham Lowe, one-third of a sample of recent university graduates were living with their parents, and the average age in the sample was over 25.[54]

American data reveal the same trend. According to a report from the William T. Grant Foundation, in 1985, "six of 10 men between the ages of 18 and 24 were living at home, compared to 52 percent in 1960. Similarly, half of women in this age group were at home, up from 35 percent in 1960."[55]

Those living with their parents this late in life have been dubbed "boomerang kids."[56]

*Unemployment.*   In Canada, the official unemployment rate for individuals aged 15 to 24 hovers at almost twice the average rate for all groups. As of 1987, in Canada, those aged 15 to 24 made up "34% of all the employed, although they accounted for only 21% of the labour force."[57] Chart 2.9 shows the consistency in the age patterning of unemployment over a 10-year period in Canada. This chart illustrates that the young are particularly affected by recessions, as was the case in the early 80s.

Table 2.3 presents more details regarding the numbers represented in chart 2.9. At the height of the recession, 1982–83, the unemployment rate was over 24 percent for males aged 15 to 19 and about 20 percent for males aged 20 to 24.[58] Young women fared somewhat better than young men, although as we see in chapter 3, they would have been paid less. Even after the economy recovered, by 1986 the unemployment rate for the 15 to 24 age group was 17 percent for men and 14 percent for women, compared with eight percent for those in

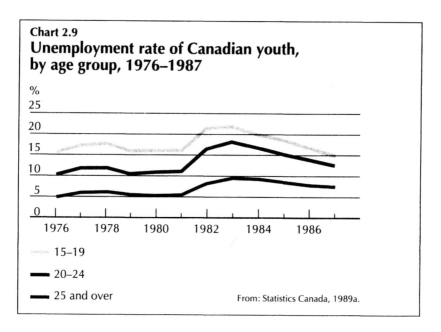

**Chart 2.9**
**Unemployment rate of Canadian youth,
by age group, 1976–1987**

15–19
20–24
25 and over

From: Statistics Canada, 1989a.

the over-25 age group. As of 1990, the overall average unemployment rate for 15- to 24-year-olds was 12.8 percent (ranging from 11.6 to 14.6 over the span of the year) compared with 8.1 percent for all persons in the labor force.[59]

We can gain a sense of the situation facing young Americans by examining the unemployment trends provided in chart 2.10. Here we see the long-term trend of greater youth unemployment over a 30-year period, as well as racial and ethnic differences. In 1986 the unemployment rate for white youths was 11.1 percent compared to 26.6 percent for black youth. As of 1988, figures were 13 and 35 percent, respectively, while the rate stood at about five percent for those over 24.[60]

Whichever way we analyze the figures, the economy is not kind to young people as a group in Canada or the United States, either in terms of providing initial employment or in terms of providing stable and rewarding employment. This statement holds true for most Western countries. For example, from a study of 10 industrialized nations (including Canada and the United States), males between the ages of 15 and 19 were reported to have an unemployment rate seven times

## Table 2.3
## Unemployment figures for Canadian youth, by age group and sex, 1976–1987

| Sex/Age | 1976 | 1977 | 1978 | 1979 | 1980 | 1981 | 1982 | 1983 | 1984 | 1985 | 1986 | 1987 |
|---|---|---|---|---|---|---|---|---|---|---|---|---|
| Male 15–19 | 16.3 | 18.1 | 18.4 | 16.3 | 17.0 | 16.9 | 24.6 | 24.2 | 21.3 | 20.6 | 18.2 | 16.4 |
| Female 15–19 | 15.1 | 16.7 | 17.1 | 15.8 | 15.3 | 15.4 | 18.9 | 20.1 | 18.5 | 16.7 | 15.2 | 13.6 |
| Male 20–24 | 11.1 | 12.6 | 12.7 | 11.0 | 11.3 | 12.2 | 19.0 | 21.4 | 18.4 | 17.0 | 15.5 | 13.9 |
| Female 20–24 | 9.8 | 11.7 | 11.5 | 10.4 | 10.7 | 10.0 | 14.4 | 15.2 | 14.9 | 13.4 | 12.9 | 11.8 |
| Male 25 + | 4.2 | 4.9 | 5.2 | 4.5 | 4.8 | 4.8 | 8.2 | 9.2 | 8.9 | 8.3 | 7.6 | 7.0 |
| Female 25 + | 6.6 | 7.4 | 7.7 | 7.0 | 6.5 | 6.7 | 8.8 | 9.6 | 9.7 | 9.4 | 8.6 | 8.4 |

Annual averages

From: Statistics Canada, 1989a.

greater than all individuals 25 years of age and older. Furthermore, as evidence that circumstances have worsened with the entrenchment of advanced industrial society, the proportion of unemployed 15- to 19-year-olds to those over 25 years went from an average of 2.5 times in 1965 to 4.0 times in 1979.[61] Similar statistics for 1989 indicate that those under 25

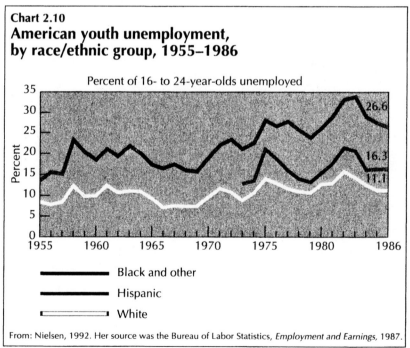

## Chart 2.10
## American youth unemployment, by race/ethnic group, 1955–1986

Percent of 16- to 24-year-olds unemployed

Black and other

Hispanic

White

From: Nielsen, 1992. Her source was the Bureau of Labor Statistics, *Employment and Earnings*, 1987.

were 2.7 times more likely to be unemployed than those over 25 in the United States, and 1.7 times more likely to be unemployed in Canada.[62]

Thus far we have referred only to the officially unemployed.[63] If we include "discouraged workers" and those forced to work sporadically and for fewer hours than they would like, these figures jump by about 50 percent.[64] Furthermore, in the early 1990s fewer Canadian young people were classified as discouraged workers than in the early 1980s, primarily because more had enrolled in postsecondary educational institutions. Ernest Akyeampong expresses this in a rather understated fashion: "With reduced or nonexistent job opportunities, many job seekers are adopting various educational strategies to improve their employment prospects."[65] In other words, they are responding to the pressures of credentialism and education inflation. More recently, Statistics Canada reported a drop in the overall unemployment rate that was due primarily to another 45,000 young people becoming discouraged workers.[66]

***Poverty.*** After reviewing the relevant statistics for Canada, David Ross and Richard Shillington conclude that there has been a "marked shift in the age distribution of poverty."[67] They base this conclusion on the observation of a fall in the overall population poverty rate between 1973 and 1986, while the poverty rate for households headed by someone under 25 almost doubled, rising from 16 percent to 30 percent. Similarly, the rate for unattached individuals in this age group increased from 40 to about 48 percent over the same period. Comparable increases occurred in the United States. As noted by the William T. Grant Foundation:

> Among families headed by a person under 25, the poverty rate almost doubled from 1973 to 1985, from 15.9 to 30.2 percent. The poverty rate of young white families doubled from 11.7 to 24.7 percent, while the rate for young black families . . . rose . . . from 42.9 percent in 1973 to 62.1 percent in 1985.[68]

Young people in Canada and the United States are not alone in the poor economic quality of life they face. Table 2.4 provides data from four major Western countries, three of which have poverty rates among the young that are about twice the rate for the general population.[69]

**Table 2.4**

## Relative rates of poverty for several countries

|  | Year | All persons | Under age 24 |
|---|---|---|---|
| Canada | 1981 | 12.1% | 22.7% |
| United Kingdom | 1979 | 8.8% | 11.6% |
| United States | 1979 | 16.9% | 28.0% |
| West Germany | 1981 | 7.2% | 14.5% |

From: Ross and Shillington, 1989.

The power wielded by various groups in a society can be seen in government policies. One such policy is the minimum wage set by the state for businesses and industries to follow. Chart 2.11 illustrates what has happened to the average minimum wage in Canada as a percentage of the poverty line over the past 20 years. The chart shows that before the 1980s working for a minimum wage in Canada guaranteed that one would not be forced to live in poverty (as defined by the statistical poverty line). Since 1980, however, this has not been the case. In fact, the situation has worsened so much that a minimum wage earner now makes only 70 percent of the poverty line (versus 137 percent of the poverty line in 1976). Thus, the economic circumstances of the economically powerless deteriorated during the 1980s. But when we look at the age dimension, we find that the majority — 64 percent — of those earning the minimum wage are between the ages of 16 and 24. In the United States in 1988, 58 percent of minimum wage earners were under 24.[70] Clearly, then, many young people are forced to live in poverty because of government policies and related business practices.

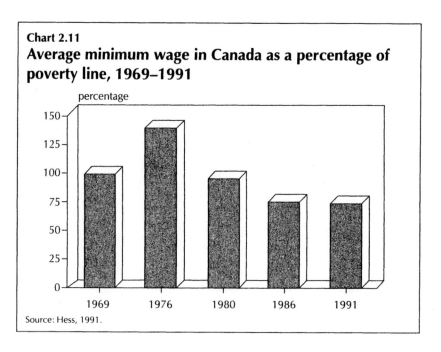

**Chart 2.11**

**Average minimum wage in Canada as a percentage of poverty line, 1969–1991**

percentage

150 —
125 —
100 —
75 —
50 —
25 —
0 —

| 1969 | 1976 | 1980 | 1986 | 1991 |

Source: Hess, 1991.

## Changes in Emotional Experiences

There are emotional costs associated with the economic plight of the young in modern Western societies, and these costs appear to be increasing. As we see, this age group suffers from a number of problems in areas of day-to-day functioning. An examination of statistics from the past three decades reveals consistent upward trends in these problems, which include suicide.

*Suicide.* In Canada, the suicide rate for teenagers increased almost fivefold between 1961 and 1981.[71] Currently, suicide is the second leading cause of death for this age group in both Canada[72] and the United States.[73] As illustrated in chart 2.12, young men seem to be particularly affected by this trend. In many countries, young women are three times more likely to attempt suicide, whereas young men are four times more likely to succeed.[74] While the general suicide rate in Canada has increased in the past 30 years, Renée Beneteau notes that the greatest increases have been among younger men; as of 1986,

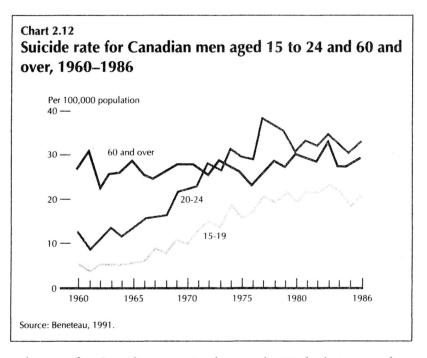

**Chart 2.12**
**Suicide rate for Canadian men aged 15 to 24 and 60 and over, 1960–1986**

Per 100,000 population

60 and over

20-24

15-19

1960    1965    1970    1975    1980    1986

Source: Beneteau, 1991.

the rate for Canadian men in their early 20s had risen to the point where it was the highest for any group except men over 70.[75] Based on American figures, David Curran reports a 72 percent rise in the rate for 15- to 19-year-olds since 1968, with rates for those in the 20 to 25 age range being twice as high.[76] David Cole notes that although the nationwide rate for all age groups has been stable in the United States for the past 30 years, the adolescent rate has tripled, rising from 4.1 per 100,000 in 1955 to 12.9 in 1985.[77] Chart 2.13 depicts this trend with a projection to the year 2000.

From a political economy perspective, one would predict that suicide rates would be higher in groups with less power, as in the case of racial and ethnic minorities, and in groups that undergo a decrease in social status, as in the case of the young and the elderly. The available statistics support this prediction. For example, in 1986 the rate for native Canadian men aged 15 to 29 was 100 per 100,000.[78] This is apparently the highest rate in the world (the rate for all native males was 56.3, two and a half times that for all males in Canada).[79]

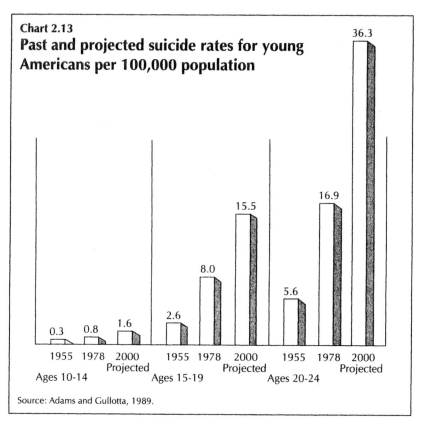

**Chart 2.13**

**Past and projected suicide rates for young Americans per 100,000 population**

36.3

16.9

15.5

8.0

5.6

2.6

0.3  0.8  1.6

| 1955 | 1978 | 2000 Projected | 1955 | 1978 | 2000 Projected | 1955 | 1978 | 2000 Projected |

Ages 10-14          Ages 15-19          Ages 20-24

Source: Adams and Gullotta, 1989.

Similarly, the suicide rate for young African-American men has tripled since 1960, while the rate for native American youths has increased tenfold in the past 20 years.[80] As in Canada, the overall suicide rate for natives is the highest of the major racial or ethnic groups, and it peaks during young adulthood.[81] Importantly, the exception to the high rate among native American youths is those who have not been as culturally disenfranchised, that is, those who observe traditional customs or who live in areas "where the opportunities for employment and education exist within the tribal community itself."[82]

While these official statistics are alarming, many experts feel that the actual rate is three times that of the official one.[83] They believe that many suicides go unrecognized or are covered up as accidents. For example, car crashes are the leading cause of death for this age group in both Canada and the

United States and can result either directly or indirectly from suicidal impulses. The statistics get even worse as we delve further into this issue. Surveys have revealed that between 10 and 15 percent of people in their teens and 20s attempt suicide at some time, while between 35 and 55 percent will admit to having thought about taking their own lives.[84] Some experts estimate that there are as many as "200 suicide attempts for every adolescent death by suicide."[85]

In short, suicide, attempted suicide, or thoughts about suicide are part of the reality that many young people face today, and the situation appears to be getting worse. These statistics can hardly be said to reflect the idea that these individuals are going through their best years. Indeed, if people were going through their best years, they would not be risking and losing their lives at such an alarming rate. Nor, as we are about to see, would they be jeopardizing their physical and mental health in such great numbers.

***Psychological Well-Being.*** Available estimates indicate that approximately 20 percent of so-called normal teenagers (that is, those who are not psychiatric patients or convicted delinquents) will admit "to feeling empty emotionally, being confused most of the time, or hearing strange noises."[86] Admitting to, in the words of psychiatrists Daniel Offer and Melvin Sabshin, such "gross psychiatric symptoms" on a questionnaire makes one wonder how many more would admit to similar problems under conditions where a clinical rapport were established. Some people might respond to this figure by saying that it underlines the storm and stress young people experience due to fluctuating hormone levels. However, when we examine the way in which the psychological world of young people has changed over the past three decades, we see an increase in problems that cannot be explained in terms of biology. Daniel Offer, a leading American psychiatrist, has collected data from the 1960s, 1970s, and 1980s that allow us to gauge how societal changes are affecting the manner in which coming of age is experienced in Western cultures.

Referring to these changes, Offer and his colleague Melvin Sabshin note that compared to adolescents from the early 1960s, those of the late 1970s and early 1980s are "less secure about their body image and self-esteem." Moreover, they "have more overt behavioral problems . . . are more worried about their future and less hopeful about their ability to function as adults." This research also indicates that in the early 1960s, young people "were less lonely and valued friendships somewhat more than do current adolescents." Finally, by the beginning of the 1980s, many teenagers believed "they should be *more* sexually active" and felt "insecure or inferior" as a result (emphasis added).[87]

From another longitudinal study, Martin Seligman has noted that "today's young [American] people [are] about 10 times as likely to be depressed as were their parents and grandparents." Seligman attributes this "epidemic of depression," as he calls it, to the tremendous expectations placed on the self to be both the source and the "architect" of most forms of gratification — to "decide, prefer, plan, and choose [its] own course of action." However, this pressure "need not lead to depression as long as we can fall back on large institutions."[88] Seligman argues that the "rampant individualism" of American society, along with a decline in commitment to common social institutions, has created this depression. With the institutions that are supposedly guiding the young into adulthood themselves in disarray, it is little wonder that the young are becoming increasingly despondent.

***Mortality and Morbidity.*** As previously mentioned, the leading cause of death of the 15- to 24-year-old group is the automobile accident — 48 per 100,000 in Canada and 52 per 100,000 in the United States.[89] Young persons are more likely to drive faster, not to wear seat belts, and to drive more closely to vehicles in front of them. Also, those aged 12 to 25 are five times more likely to use street drugs than those over 25. Finally, the 15- to 25-year-old group are arrested for a disproportionate number of crimes, especially violent crimes and ones involving property.[90]

Some would say that these statistics merely confirm the belief that these people are biologically immature and therefore incapable of controlling their impulses or handling responsibility. Perhaps, but this line of reasoning, which assumes some sort of developmental deficiency in young people created by a hormonal imbalance, cannot account for the fact that the same statistics show that in the last 30 to 40 years, all these behaviors have become much more common. With this in view, if one were to stick with an argument based on the notion of a developmental deficiency, one would have to assume that young people somehow changed genetically during this time. Furthermore, such an argument does not explain dramatic increases in crime rates in countries like the United States. For example, Jeffrey Arnett reviews studies that show an 800 percent increase in drunk driving arrests for Americans 18 to 24 years of age between 1965 and 1985, and a tenfold increase in the arrest rate for persons aged 14 to 24 between 1950 and 1985 (from 10 per 1,000 to 100 per 1,000).[91] Table 2.5 shows the increase in the overall arrest rate in the United States between 1950 and 1988. More recent American figures reveal a sharp rise in arrests related to violent crimes: between 1987 and 1991, murder arrests of juveniles (aged 10 to 17) increased by 85 percent and weapons violations increased by 62 percent.[92]

**Table 2.5**
**Arrests per 1,000 young persons in the United States, 1950–1990**

|  | Age | |
| --- | --- | --- |
|  | **14–17** | **18–25** |
| 1950 | 4 | 13 |
| 1960 | 47 | 42 |
| 1970 | 104 | 74 |
| 1980 | 126 | 114 |
| 1990 | 117 | 117 |

Source: Howe and Strauss, 1993.

In fact, young Americans *inherited* a culture of violence; they did not create it. Today, American adolescents are twice as likely to be victims of violent crimes than are adults. Homicide is now the leading cause of death among African-American adolescent males and the third leading cause of death for all adolescents.[93] Twenty years ago street gangs used switchblades and iron pipes as weapons. Now automatic guns are not uncommon. The young do not manufacture these weapons; rather, they buy them from adults who are licensed by the state to sell them. The availability of these weapons is partly responsible for the fact that five percent of African-American males will be murdered. In one year alone, more young black males are murdered than were killed in almost 10 years of fighting in Vietnam.[94] Black youths are six times more likely to be murder victims than white ones, and are three times more likely to be arrested for weapons offenses.[95] The crime cycle they are caught up in means they have a greater chance of going to prison than to college. Indeed, one in four African Americans "between the ages of 20 and 29 is currently in prison, on probation, or on parole."[96] According to the same source, this figure is four in 10 in urban areas.[97]

The general public tends to believe that it is natural for young people to experience the circumstances and behaviors we have just examined. Adults do not take youths seriously or treat them with due respect because they believe that they are not mature enough to look after themselves properly or to make responsible decisions. This is especially the case for those still in their teen years. The problem with this line of reasoning is that most young people are no longer given opportunities to assume roles that would help them to learn how to act maturely and responsibly. Instead, they are kept financially and emotionally dependent on adults, mainly on their parents or on surrogate parents such as teachers, who have been given control by the state over their lives. As we argue, this condition of forced financial and emotional dependency and a concomitant erosion of rights and social status appears to be augmenting so much that it is no longer clear when an individual is an adult as opposed to a young person. As Gary Melton writes, in the United States a "17-year-old, like a 17-day-old, is a legal 'infant.'"[98]

Thus far, we have presented a rather sterile statistical portrait of contemporary youth. To bring this portrait to life, we have added a passionate plea from a teenager whose daily life reflects many of the problems that beset the young. In her words:

> Today's teen-agers are a minority that suffers major discrimination. Most teen-agers do not have the right to vote. They are not represented in government. They have legal identity only through their parents. Teen-agers are often paid less than adults even though the jobs are the same. Many stores do not allow more than one teen-ager inside at a time. Many restaurants do not allow teens to sit in certain areas.

> Society continually concentrates on negatives when it comes to teen-agers. . . . What are adults afraid of? Why are responsible, respectable — if young — Canadians ostracized, ignored and shunned . . . ?

> Society needs to recognize that it is not fair to apply stereotypes to teen-agers. People tend to live up to the expectations of others, and once society starts recognizing the positive contributions of adolescents, teens will not longer need to find other means of gaining recognition and attention.

> Adults need to encourage teen-agers to channel their energies into worthwhile projects. By concentrating on the positives rather than the negatives, society would treat teen-agers as valuable citizens rather than lost causes. . . . If today's teen-agers see themselves as responsible, worthwhile citizens, Canada can only benefit.[99]

# THE DISENFRANCHISEMENT OF YOUTH

When we evaluate the statistical evidence presented above with the theoretical perspectives discussed in the last chapter, it becomes apparent that the political economy view most completely accounts for recent changes in the circumstances confronting young people. Clearly, each theory can account in part for what has happened, but we believe the latter view is the most comprehensive and astute, particularly insofar as it connects the declining fortunes of the young with the increasing fortunes of older people. Indeed, the data analyzed above pertaining to wages, poverty, unemployment, and underemployment in Canada and the United States consistently point to the fact that young persons are being sequestered in the educational system for increasingly long periods and that they are also being exploited in the workplace. Closely tied to this phenomenon is a redistribution of wealth, with age as a primary axis. Thus, in advanced industrial society the young are increasingly being used as a source of cheap surplus labor and have lost the status and independence they might have enjoyed in earlier times. Due to this army of cheap labor, prices in certain sectors of the economy have fallen and corporate profits have risen, as have the salaries of some adults.

This redistribution of wealth can be seen as part of a behind-the-scenes power struggle of which many people are unaware. But in this power struggle, those in the younger age groups are almost entirely unrepresented, while those in the older ones are making the decisions, many of which are heavily in their favor. The cumulative weight of these decisions, encouraged by prejudices regarding the nature of youth, has legitimated the exploitation of the young so that few question it. Consequently, those running businesses and corporations have found a cheap supply of labor, and they have taken full advantage of it.

As is often the case, the least desirable jobs go to those with the least power in a society. While the dimensions of power have long been thought of along the lines of race, gender, and class, what these data indicate is that age, or more specifically youth, is an increasingly important component of power and therefore economic and social franchise. It is also the case that once a job becomes predominantly associated with low-status individuals, the pay drops along with benefits and job security. Businesses and corporations have both contributed to and capitalized on the diminishing social status of young people by restructuring jobs and reducing salaries. The best example of this is fast-food chain restaurants. Now, when looking for work, young persons often have no choice but to take such jobs, which are usually below minimum wage, part-time, with few benefits and little opportunity for career advancement. It is part and parcel of discrimination against youths that these practices are seen to be normal and fair, even by many of those who say they speak for equal opportunities for all groups in society. When ethnic groups or women are the targets of occupational ghettoization, the unfairness of the practice is much more likely to gain public and academic attention.

While businesses and corporations benefit from the disenfranchisement of youth, the above data suggest that older age groups also benefit at the expense of their younger colleagues. Notwithstanding unemployment and underemployment problems that all age groups face, persons aged 35 and over are more likely to be established in careers and naturally presume that they are entitled to *more* pay, benefits, and security. Because more older people are in positions of influence, they can establish how much they are financially rewarded for their labor and how much, or little, others are rewarded. They appear to have been giving themselves an increasing share of the pie, and their juniors a decreasing share, thereby taking advantage of the latter group's vulnerability.[100]

What is taking place is more than a simple competition for resources between the baby boomers and "baby-busters." For example, the Canadian population aged 16 to 24 dropped from 4,200,000 to 3,800,000 between 1981 and 1986. As Wannell observes, "it might be expected that reduced labour force competition resulting from a smaller population, combined with rising educational attainment, would *increase* youth wages" (emphasis added).[101] His figures reveal that the opposite took place.[102] The fact that the youth segment is no longer as large, particularly in relation to baby boomers, has undoubtedly affected policy-making, explaining some of the older generation's inattention to problems faced by youths.

We believe, however, that government policies are chiefly affected by transformations in the economy. If we return to chart 2.7, we can see that it bears this out. Note that as of 1986, economic benefits accrued to both over-35 groups. In 1986, the baby-boom cohort would have ranged from 30 to 40 years old, yet those older than the baby boomers were also thriving, so something other than a mere pampering of baby boomers is going on.

As we argue in part 2, the circumstances imposed on young people are beginning to resemble those portrayed in Aldous Huxley's *Brave New World*. That is, in "conjunction with the freedom to daydream under the influence of dope and movies and the radio" it is necessary to reconcile young people "to the servitude which is their fate."[103] As in Huxley's dystopia, in our society social control measures have been used to elicit the conformity of the young — to manufacture their consent to participate in a capitalist society. Huxley writes that "without economic security, the love of servitude cannot possibly come into existence."[104] As we have seen in this chapter, this condition is not fully met in contemporary society. Since the rewards offered for conformity are becoming insufficient compensation for the punishments meted out, the young are less accepting of their disenfranchised position in today's world.

The overall quality of life and psychological well-being of the young has deteriorated. The political economy perspective connects this deterioration with the fact that youths have been manipulated by various identity-forming industries and leisure industries. The latter exploit young people's sexuality, beliefs about femininity and masculinity, and their insecurities to sell their products. Advertising campaigns often make teenagers believe they are inadequate if they do not look the right way and consume or do the right things, the latter being defined by the captains of these industries.[105] These deteriorations cannot be attributed to some suddenly acquired biological deficiency among the young since the 1950s, but rather must be attributed to changes in the socioeconomic circumstances confronting them.

# 3

## The Conquest of Youth

While it was not Erik Erikson's intention to develop a sociology of youth, this psychoanalyst's work is useful in making links between macro, sociological concepts and micro, psychological ones.[1] In making these links we return to Margaret Mead's idea that the way in which a culture structures coming-of-age processes has a direct bearing on how youth is experienced. Erikson believed this as well and proposed that cultures can precipitate, aggravate, and prolong identity crises.[2] However, Erikson did not lay out the details of the cultural conditions under which this happens, so we will venture to do so here.

From a cross-cultural, transhistorical point of view, the cultural definition of coming of age often depends on the needs and the level of affluence of a given culture. For example, if its viability depends on all its members contributing their labor, people will tend to be recruited from childhood to adulthood, so there will be little or no period of adolescence. These cultures generally use the labor of children and simply increase the work requirement after puberty, when they have a greater physical capacity. To hasten the coming-of-age process, these cultures often rely on puberty rites or rites of passage to confer adult status.

Because roles are clearly defined in these cultures, the stresses associated with entering adulthood in Western societies are minimal. When occupational roles require more lengthy training or apprenticeships, the period of adolescence tends to be prolonged accordingly, introducing condition that might give rise to a stressful transition to adulthood.[3]

The cultural definition of coming of age also depends on the stability and coherence of the culture in question. If a culture is going through rapid changes or is otherwise unstable, an ambivalence toward the young can develop. As the identity of adult members becomes ambiguous, they are less able to guide the young through the self-discovery process that is an integral part of forming an identity. Consequently, they may feel alienated from their juniors, and be less likely to welcome them into adult society. This ambivalence could precipate a crisis among the young.

The cultural definition of coming of age can also depend on the ethos of the culture. For example, if it is predicated on the notion of survival of the fittest, an ethos that ignores values like caring and sharing, the young will be judged in those terms. Moreover, if adults are excessively self-interested, they will tend to be more rejecting of the young. Finally, such a society is more likely to produce young people who are confused about themselves and how they should go about coming of age. This brings us back to Erikson.

## THE PSYCHOLOGICAL BASIS OF IDENTITY

Before considering Erikson's identity theory, it is instructive to examine some of his basic assumptions and concepts. Erikson is considered by many to be the foremost theorist of human development of the latter part of the 20th century. He came of age himself under the tutelage of Sigmund Freud and Freud's daughter Anna. Yet in his own work he has gone beyond Freudian theory in several important respects.[4] First, he has outlined how development after childhood takes place in a variety of meaningful ways and argues that some individuals can actually remake their personalities by exploring previous difficulties. Second, unlike Freud, who focuses on the darker aspects of the mind such as incestuous fantasies and neurosis, Erikson concentrates on the positive components of the psyche, including creativity, adaptation, altruism, dedication, and ethical striving.

In Erikson's view, humans are not condemned to be prisoners of their animal instincts or early environment. Instead, he believes that as they pass through the life cycle and encounter the challenges of life all humans have the capacity to be agentic meaning-seekers who can strive to know the unknowable and do the "undoable." But for this capacity to emerge fully, culture must encourage it. Finally, for Erikson, the social world is not inevitably an oppressive monolith as Freud tended to view it; rather, it can be benign and facilitative and provide a place in which personal fulfillment and development can be nurtured. In sum, Erikson has given psychoanalytic thought an optimistic alternative to Freud's rather gloomy and pessimistic view of the world.

Erikson has maintained several essential components of Freud's psychology, particularly those related to the structure of the psyche, or mind. According to Erikson's theory, the human potential to develop competencies associated with being an active social agent is determined by the *ego*. In his sense of the term, the ego designates a set of mental processes that are created by *dialectic tensions*. These tensions are initially manifested in the attempts of infants to overcome the obstacles that stand in the way of their basic desires for nourishment and comfort. As infants become young children, their egos grow on the basis of the synthesis of certain types of competency-oriented tensions associated with the meeting of their needs and desires in ways considered appropriate by their culture; without these tensions, their egos become passive and weak. These tensions must be meaningful, rather than simply being conflicts between random impulses and arbitrary obstacles. As the ego determines the meaning of the tensions it experiences, or *synthesizes* experiences, it becomes more able to overcome those tensions, that is, to *execute* behaviors. In turn, the increased facility in ego-synthesizing and -executing functions assists the ego in moving to a more advanced level of development. It is this movement through increasingly advanced levels of ego mastery to which Erikson refers when he speaks of his eight stages of psychosocial development.[5]

If the ego is prevented from actively engaging with its environment or if it attempts to deal with tasks at too advanced a level, the ensuing frustration can damage it, especially if the frustration continues for a period and/or lacks meaning for the ego. This is precisely the position that we put many young people in when we subject them to long periods of childlike dependency and marginalization; for instance, in the many educational institutions that discourage ego-mastery for prolonged periods because their primary concern is with disciplining and controlling their wards. Ego-mastery is also hampered when we subject people to enforced idleness, as in the case of un- and underemployment. In these situations, we set the stage for regressive behavior on a mass scale by handcuffing the ego and invalidated much of the meaning it might create for itself. When frustrated in this way, some young people turn to gratifying their immediate impulses, a behavior that is now widespread and difficult to reverse in adulthood. As we see in part 2, this self-defeating tendency is complementary to the dominant economic and political interests that prevail in advanced industrial society.

In addition to his conception of the ego, Erikson developed the more specific notion of *ego identity*, which helps us to understand the coming-of-age process. In developing this concept, Erikson was concerned with how individuals maintain or lose their sense of continuity as individuals over time and through social situations. He came to realize the importance of temporal-spatial continuity when treating shell-shocked soldiers during World War II. Erikson came to view these people not as exhibiting some organic psychopathology, but instead as experiencing an identity crisis brought on by the "exigencies of war," which caused them to lose their "sense of personal sameness and historical continuity." He drew a parallel between traumatized war victims and "severely conflicted young people whose sense of confusion is due . . . to a war within themselves." He believed that the same psychological mechanisms were at work for those who had "lost themselves" as a result of traumatic wartime experiences and those who have difficulties making the transition from childhood to adulthood.[6]

After studying how different cultures deal with the transition between childhood and adulthood, Erikson noted that cultures vary in the forms of guidance and support they provide to lessen the trauma and stress associated with the metamorphosis of the child into an adult. This notion of guidance and support is embodied in Erikson's notion of the *psychosocial moratorium*. We will use the more specific term *identity moratorium* to designate the time-out imposed on adolescents and youth during which they are supposedly expected to sort out the components that will constitute their adult identity. From Erikson's perspective, these identity moratoria should function to lessen the trauma of the identity transformation experience during the coming-of-age period.

## ADOLESCENCE AS A MORATORIUM

Individuals experiencing an identity moratorium in advanced industrial societies often seek out formally structured institutional settings, such as schools which provide them with a time-out from the tasks of adulthood. This ostensibly enables them to develop themselves on a personal level and to explore possible career paths. In theory, identity moratoria can provide young people with opportunities to experiment with roles, ideas, beliefs, and life-styles and can set them on a life course that is rich and rewarding. During this period, individuals can undo old psychological problems and start life afresh.[7]

While these good things can and do happen among the more fortunate and privileged, in reality what we find is that many people get lost, sidetracked, and confused in this identity moratorium. Consequently, this may end up being the most destructive or wasted period of their lives, something that is particularly true for those who cannot use the time to explore their identity due to limited financial resources. Clearly, many young people from racial and ethnic minorities and the lower classes cannot afford the luxury of an identity crisis that involves elaborate forms of self-exploration, such as world travel or experimenting with different schools and academic majors. Instead, their time-out, which often takes place in the same community in which they were born and will live as adults, provides little opportunity or guidance.

Still, some individuals are able to create their own moratorium and to benefit from it. For example, travelling with knapsack on back is a time-honored moratorium (Erikson himself did this). Whether the trip be completely unstructured or well planned, it reflects the individual's need to explore him- or herself in a way that cannot be done in mainstream society.

Other youths experience difficulties during their time-out, particularly when they are not supported in their need to explore themselves. Such individuals often stagnate or drift; they may develop mechanisms that shut the world out and occlude possibilities for self-growth. Some of these people fit into those pockets of adult society filled with adults who did the same thing. Those who do not will have a difficult time and often end up turning to the more extreme form of youth subcultures. Indeed, for many, these subcultures constitute a type of moratorium, in the sense that they negate their parents' values. In some cases, it appears that these subcultures can foster ego development and the individual may eventually outgrow them.[8] In other cases, though, these subcultures become a permanent life-style or even a death trap.

For those who cannot make their own moratorium and who burden the system by deviating in various ways, numerous bureaucracies are poised and ready for action. Indeed, it can be argued that an attempt has been made to bureaucratize nonconformity among this segment of the population as a means of handling the fallout from the marginalization imposed on them. For minor deviations, which often constitute violations of the work ethic, there are bureaucracies that provide alternating unemployment benefits and work programs. This form of control prevents many young persons from engaging in more threatening deviations such as robberies, but it also locks them into a role of dependency on the state. Being dependent on the state, however, they are less likely to question the impact of its policies on their lives. The state often tolerates the continual petty deviations of these individuals because they do not constitute challenges to the economic system but rather are related to the hedonism of their marginalized life-style.

For major deviations, bureaucracies are in place that not only monitor an individual's behavior but also seek to correct it. For those who have become so alienated from society that they do not care about the consequences of their actions, psychiatric hospitals and prisons exist, which by all accounts are bursting at their seams in North America. (These institutions also serve as a warning for those who are tempted to test the limits of acceptable deviance.) Ironically, as Erikson points out, at this extreme point of alienation an extremely structured situation is imposed on the individual, and this structure provides a much needed identity moratorium, albeit one that confers a negative identity. For some, this type of moratorium may be therapeutic and the individual may find her or his way out of the dilemma. However, others may permanently adopt the identity that is conferred upon them in this setting and in so doing block the possibility of developing a more positive self-image.

Erikson has repeatedly warned about the permanent harm that can be done when official labels are placed on individuals, particularly when these individuals are merely experimenting with their identity.[9] Labels like "delinquent" and "psychiatric patient" often serve only to reinforce what is to be "corrected." Erikson further argues that many of the problems facing such individuals are better conceptualized as the result of identity problems, and the cure lies not in reinforcing a negative identity, but in nurturing a positive one.

While the young person can get lost and confused when experiencing an identity moratorium, from an Eriksonian perspective, the moratorium can potentially provide a tremendous opportunity for self-discovery. The exploration and experimentation that is undertaken during this time can set the individual on a life course that is rich and rewarding. Whether this period is a benefit or a liability has much to do with a person's environment. If the environment nurtures the individual's capacities and encourages self-discovery instead of stifling these things, it can enrich one's life.

We dealt extensively in the last chapter with the declining economic circumstances facing young people and how this situation is worse for youths who belong to racial or ethnic minorities. Clearly, there are limitations to the opportunities that various segments of the youth population have in terms of participating in established moratoria. By way of further illustration, table 3.1 provides a breakdown of college participation rates according to class, race, and gender. While women appear to fare better at the college level (56.4 percent of those in the United States participate), as discussed below this advantage does not always translate into tangible benefits. In table 3.2, for example, it can be seen that women's participation in the more highly rewarded science and engineering programs is far less than that of males. The extreme underrepresentation of racial minorities is especially striking in this table.

In Canada, native youths are having a particularly difficult time.[10] For example, formal schooling appears to provide few rewards or incentives. As David Ross reports,

> many Indian children are raised in an economic environment some people would consider hopeless. In 1986, for example, the average employment income of Indians who were 15 to 24 years old and who had high school education was $4,676, For those with less than nine years of education it was only $700 less, hardly an inducement not to drop out. The unemployment rate for all Indians on reserves (15 years plus) was 35 per cent. And over half (57 per cent) were not even in the labour force.[11]

**Table 3.1**

## College participation rates of 18- to 24-year-olds in the United States by income, race, and sex, 1973 to 1988

| Income, Race, and Sex | 1973 | 1976 | 1979 | 1982 | 1985 | 1987 | 1988 |
|---|---|---|---|---|---|---|---|
| **White** | | | | | | | |
| **Total** | **47.9%** | **49.3%** | **46.2%** | **46.3%** | **47.3%** | **50.9%** | **52.9%** |
| Low | 36.8 | 37.0 | 35.8 | 32.5 | 31.7 | 36.4 | 38.8 |
| Middle | 44.5 | 46.0 | 43.1 | 42.3 | 46.0 | 48.7 | 51.0 |
| Upper | 59.9 | 60.9 | 56.4 | 59.3 | 57.2 | 62.0 | 63.2 |
| **Men** | **48.1** | **46.1** | **44.5** | **43.8** | **44.7** | **50.9** | **49.8** |
| Low | 37.9 | 34.9 | 33.8 | 29.9 | 29.1 | 36.4 | 32.1 |
| Middle | 44.2 | 42.4 | 41.6 | 39.5 | 43.0 | 48.4 | 48.8 |
| Upper | 60.2 | 57.3 | 53.6 | 56.7 | 55.0 | 62.0 | 60.6 |
| **Women** | **47.5** | **53.3** | **48.2** | **49.3** | **50.4** | **52.6** | **56.4** |
| Low | 35.4 | 39.4 | 38.1 | 35.3 | 34.8 | 38.0 | 46.4 |
| Middle | 44.9 | 50.5 | 44.6 | 45.5 | 49.4 | 49.9 | 53.5 |
| Upper | 59.4 | 65.5 | 60.1 | 62.4 | 60.0 | 64.8 | 66.1 |
| **African American** | | | | | | | |
| **Total** | **33.2** | **47.5** | **39.0** | **36.0** | **32.8** | **37.1** | **35.5** |
| Low | 31.7 | 39.8 | 34.2 | 29.2 | 27.9 | 31.1 | 30.3 |
| Middle | 32.0 | 52.7 | 43.6 | 40.2 | 35.5 | 39.3 | 36.2 |
| Upper | * | * | * | * | * | * | * |
| **Men** | **34.9** | **46.5** | **36.4** | **32.6** | **30.8** | **35.1** | **29.5** |
| Low | * | 37.2 | 36.1 | 23.0 | 29.0 | 26.8 | 23.0 |
| Middle | * | 53.2 | 36.4 | 39.4 | 29.0 | 37.4 | 28.1 |
| Upper | * | * | * | * | * | * | * |
| **Women** | **31.6** | **48.3** | **41.4** | **39.1** | **34.6** | **38.8** | **40.8** |
| Low | * | 41.7 | 32.9 | 34.2 | 27.1 | 34.1 | 35.6 |
| Middle | * | 52.2 | 51.0 | 41.0 | 42.6 | 41.0 | 44.1 |
| Upper | * | * | * | * | * | * | * |

* The number of cases in the sample is too small to produce reliable estimates for this population.

From: Nielsen, 1992. Her source was the American Council on Education, Status Report on Minorities in Education, 1988.

**Table 3.2**

## Who got science and engineering degrees in the United States?

| Year and Group | | Bachelor's | | Master's | | Ph.D. | |
|---|---|---|---|---|---|---|---|
| | | Number | % | Number | % | Number | % |
| Total | 1985 | 204,064 | 100.0 | 43,910 | 100.0 | 11,821 | 100.0 |
| | 1987 | 203,055 | 100.0 | 47,947 | 100.0 | 13,040 | 100.0 |
| Women | 1985 | 62,448 | 30.6 | 9,724 | 22.1 | 2,135 | 18.1 |
| | 1987 | 61,487 | 30.3 | 11,443 | 23.9 | 2,442 | 18.7 |
| African | 1985 | 8,019 | 3.9 | 788 | 1.8 | 133 | 1.1 |
| Americans | 1987 | 9,205 | 4.5 | 1,055 | 2.2 | 137 | 1.1 |
| Hispanics | 1985 | 4,613 | 2.3 | 688 | 1.5 | 218 | 1.8 |
| | 1987 | 5,266 | 2.6 | 954 | 2.0 | 217 | 1.7 |
| American | 1985 | 656 | 0.3 | 108 | 0.2 | 13 | 0.1 |
| Indians | 1987 | 662 | 0.3 | 91 | 0.2 | 15 | 0.1 |
| Asians | 1985 | 9,903 | 4.9 | 2,631 | 6.0 | 619 | 5.2 |
| | 1987 | 13,112 | 6.5 | 3,239 | 6.8 | 662 | 5.1 |
| Minority | 1985 | 23,191 | 11.4 | 4,195 | 9.6 | 983 | 8.3 |
| Subtotal | 1987 | 28,245 | 13.9 | 5,339 | 11.1 | 1,031 | 7.9 |
| Foreign | 1985 | 10,628 | 5.2 | 9,638 | 21.9 | 2,878 | 24.3 |
| | 1987 | 11,345 | 5.6 | 11,557 | 24.1 | 4,054 | 31.3 |

Includes agriculture, natural resources, computer and information sciences, life sciences, mathematics, physical sciences, and engineering.

From: Nielsen, 1992. Her source was the U.S. Department of Education, Degrees and Other Formal Awards Conferred, 1988.

Consequently, the high-school drop-out rate is about 70 percent among registered Indian youth in Canada. As Ross reports:

> [O]ver 75 per cent of reserve Indians between the ages of 15 and 34 have not finished high school. For 1990, there were about 69,000 young adult Indians (aged 15 to 34 years) on reserves who had not completed high school. Less than 10 per cent of reserve Indians aged 15 to 34

years have a trade certificate or university degree. Métis, Inuit and non-status Indians (MIN) stay in school longer than on-reserve Indians, but not as long as non-aboriginal Canadians in general. . . .[12]

The situation is worse for many Canadian native youths living in the North. There is little opportunity for them to explore themselves and to grow during adolescence, so many take extreme measures in the hope of exercising at least some control over their futures. Journalist Geoffrey York reports that some native youths routinely commit crimes in order to escape the dreariness of life in isolated northern communities:

> For many native youths in the North, a run at crime is a deliberate attempt to get caught. A trip to a southern reformatory is the easiest way to leave their isolated communities, and a criminal offence provides the ticket. Airfare south is almost impossible for a young native to afford. And a term in a Winnipeg reformatory is actually more attractive than a life of poverty and joblessness in the North. On some reserves, more than half of the crimes are committed by young people who want to leave. . . .[13]

York goes on to note that on one northern reserve "the crime rate was about four times higher than the national average." He also quotes an RCMP officer who says that "If we don't catch them, they come to us and turn themselves in. . . . It's just a way out."[14] We could cite scores of similar reports, but readers have only to read their newspapers or tune into the news to see how bleak the native predicament is.

As we have seen, when identity is in moratorium, it is open to change. We now turn to an examination of how this openness is manipulated by others.

## IDENTITY MANIPULATION

The notion of ego identity formation is central to Erikson's understanding of human development, as we have already indicated. The identity of the ego begins to be formed early in childhood as the infant's ego gains a strength that permits a continuity of autonomous functioning through time and across situations. However, because of the marginalization of the child and adolescent in many Western societies, individuals commonly confront the conditions of puberty and beyond with a relatively weak ego and a tenuous sense of identity. And, as we have argued, an inadequate identity moratorium can often make matters worse.

The marginality of the adolescent world creates tremendous challenges for those who must live in it. As we have noted, from an Eriksonian perspective, this is especially the case for a person with a relatively weak ego and a tenuous sense of identity, because he or she must now synthesize conflicting information and execute behaviors in ambiguous and often hostile situations. At this stage of the life cycle, certain influences will shape and fundamentally change the young person's belief systems and life-styles.

Adolescence is the critical period during which societies ostensibly confer the stamp of an adult identity on their young members through various rites of passage. In preindustrial and tribal societies, which tend to be more clearly structured, this stamp of adulthood usually provides an unambiguous belief system and life-style, so the issue of ego strength is much less important than, say, physical strength. In advanced industrial societies people appear to have become more symbol-oriented in the sense that they define themselves and others more by how they look and what they appear to believe than by what they do. Young persons have responded to this trend in various ways. For example, it is increasingly important for them to make statements regarding what they want others to think they believe. They often make these statements through their clothing, hairstyles, and cosmetics, all of which contain a code that can only be properly interpreted by those in the know. Those who cannot interpret the code provide a convenient "out group" upon which to heap disdain.

Such fashion codes and trends have been with us since the rise of mass culture in the 1950s, and in this regard Western society has thus been dubbed an "identity society."[15] From a postmodern perspective, more recent trends affecting the young have resulted in the deconstruction of old categories of thought so that the young person emerging from childhood with a vulnerable ego and an unformulated identity faces an ambiguous and often frightening world. The young person longs to find a niche in this world and to be accepted, but just how one becomes acceptable is often not clear. It is in part this desire not to be out of place in such an ambiguous world that leaves the young vulnerable to emotional and economic exploitation by schools, peers and, in particular, capitalist enterprises.

From both a postmodern and a political economy perspective, the paramount problem the young person faces today in many advanced industrial societies is how to formulate a viable and stable identity under uncertain and even hostile circumstances. As we saw in chapters 1 and 2, young people, especially teenagers, have limited legal rights and economic resources; they are not considered to be fully responsible for their actions and are generally treated as incomplete human beings. But, as we noted in our discussion of Erikson's theory, the ego normally grows and remains strong by *acting* in the social world in a meaningful and socially accepted manner. Many young people, however, are denied this. Thus, they often face the dilemma of having to develop a sense of identity — a sense of temporal and spatial continuity — without the proper resources. Herein lies the link between the micro social-psychological perspective based on Erikson's work and the macro sociological perspectives, particularly the political economy view.

In order to see themselves as meaningful and active agents in the world, young people must be able to project themselves into a future where they assume adult roles. If they can visualize such a viable future for themselves, they will be able to function in an autonomous, self-directed manner. Since many youths have trouble doing this, they experience a confusion of identity. The longer they experience this confusion, the more difficult it becomes to develop the ego strength necessary to enact adult roles. Thus they find themselves caught in a vicious circle that may ultimately incapacitate them or lead them to high levels of risk-taking and gratuitous violence.[16]

The high psychological casualty rates among young people that we saw in chapter 2 are connected to this identity confusion. Chronic identity confusion can produce a perpetual adolescence, which can actually replace an individual's adulthood. This condition is characterized by a refusal to assume any role that involves responsibility. In fact, a Protean type of personality has become increasingly common among adults. The latter is characterized by a continual change in life-styles and a tendency to avoid making commitments.[17]

We have just described the social-psychological or micro side of the identity manipulation equation. By applying a macro sociological perspective to these formulations, we can gain a sense of some of the causes of the difficulties many young people face in trying to make it through the moratorium imposed upon them. For example, if we change the language we have been using, we gain an insight into the implications of the objective conditions (material or economic reality) facing many young people. When we speak of a moratorium, or a delay, we are also speaking of the possibility of a disenfranchisement, because something has been taken away to produce the postponement of adulthood. When we speak of personal development or experimentation, we can also speak of the possibility of emotional vulnerability and economic exploitation. Hence, sociologically speaking, we can examine adolescence and youth in terms of possible forms of identity manipulation.

The search for causes of identity manipulation begins with the distribution of power, particularly economic power. The perspective that best accounts for the use of power is the political economy view, which we develop more fully in part 2. For the remainder of this chapter, we examine a form of identity manipulation that strikes at the heart of Western culture while serving dominant economic interests.

# GENDER INTENSIFICATION

A prominent feature of identity manipulation in many advanced industrial societies is the differential socialization of young males and females into the *ideology of gender*.[18] In speaking of the latter term, we refer to the exaggerated notions associated with the different roles that still hold many men and women in separate spheres of endeavor.[19]

While progress has been made in desegregating men and women in terms of domestic and public spheres (many women now work outside the home), this progress has been relatively slow, and in some ways appears to be stalled. Indeed, a certain amount of role segregation persists despite the fact that in the advanced industrial economy physical strength is no longer relevant for most jobs, *and* despite the fact that we now know that few *substantial* biological differences exist between men and women with respect to cognitive abilities, personality traits, or behavioral dispositions.[20]

Twenty years of research has revealed that most gender differences disappear when socialization factors are taken into account. The few remaining differences could be biological in origin (the definitive study controlling all social factors has yet to be conducted), but their origin is of little practical importance because the magnitude of these differences is so small. Variables that represent verbal and mathematic abilities, visual/spatial abilities, and aggression all remain statistically significant when males and females are compared, even when other variables are taken into account. However, it must be stressed that the difference between females and males as groups is only in the magnitude of a few percentage points. In other words, knowing someone's score on, say, a mathematics test, gives you virtually no clue as to whether or not the test writer was male or female.[21] Clearly, males and females are far more similar than they are different in terms of their cognitive abilities, character traits, and behavioral capacities. Moreover, even if the differences were greater than scientific findings indicate, these would not justify the fact, for example, that males "hold more than 80 percent of the jobs in engineering and the natural sciences."[22] Besides, though research indicates that women have slightly higher verbal abilities, they certainly do not constitute 80 percent of writers, poets, broadcasters, politicians, all professions in which good verbal skills are essential.

The most plausible explanation for the continued segregation of males and females is that an ideology of gender persists that falsely promotes the view that biological differences justify traditional gender roles. As we discuss in part 2, ideologies emphasize some things and play down others. In the case of gender comparisons, these biases have been referred to as *alpha biases* and *beta biases*.[23] The former exaggerate differences between males and females (e.g., cognitive abilities), while the latter minimize or deny differences (e.g., the extent of discrimination or segregation in the workplace). Together, these biases bolster the ideology that sustains traditional gender roles and prevent full equality between men and women.

The lack of full gender equality and desegregation can be explained in part by the gender intensification process that occurs during adolescence and youth. During this period, schools and the mass media furnish young people with attitudinal and behavioral "scripts" based on the ideology of gender.[24] But these scripts are outdated and belong to a society that is no longer sustainable. At the peak of industrialization, the traditional nuclear family prevailed with its segregated gender roles, which dictated that women should remain at home and men should go out to work. In advanced industrial society, this model has become untenable since many women have joined the labor force. As we argue further on, this outdated gendering process is perpetuated by the educational system and exploited by business enterprises, such as the mass media and the fashion, sports, and music industries. These industries sell young females goods and services based on the traditional feminine identity and pitch goods and services based on the masculine identity at young men.[25] In short, gender is "big business," so capital has a vested interest in exaggerating conceptions of gender.

This orchestration follows the principles of identity manipulation outlined in the previous section, but in this case females are more exploited than males, as we shall see. What distinguishes the gender intensification process from other identity manipulation processes is that the former frequently stimulates a "flight into femininity" for young women[26] and a "flight into masculinity" for young men.[27] The ultimate result of this process is that men and women still assume traditional and semitraditional gender roles during adulthood: men end up dominating major political and economic institutions and women ultimately adopt supportive roles. If they choose to enter the workforce, their labor is underrewarded, and if they remain at home, their work often goes unrecognized. In both cases, capital is the beneficiary in the maintenance of traditional gender roles.

Our examination of the gender intensification process begins with childhood. As children, males and females in most Western societies have a certain amount of leeway in crossing gender roles. Girls especially have this latitude and can engage in what are considered male-appropriate behaviors. When they do so, they simply acquire the label of tomboy.[28] However, the physical changes associated with puberty and the social expectations that accompany adolescence create a rigidity in gender roles in the sense that "crossover" behavior now becomes unacceptable at this stage. It is discouraged socially and even feared personally by those in their teen years.[29]

Some may find this hard to swallow in light of the prevalent belief that men and women now enjoy near-equal status in modern Western societies. However, recent studies show that we have not yet attained parity between the sexes, particularly when it comes to attitudes. For instance, on the basis of her review of the relevant literature, Linda Nielsen concludes that while some changes in gender-role attitudes have taken place among American adolescents, "the research shows that the changes lag behind what we might assume on the basis of our society's presumed support for less restrictive roles." She cites, for example, a recent study of 3,000 high-school seniors in the United States in which 85 percent "disapproved of a woman's being the breadwinner while her husband stayed home to raise the children." In addition, "more than two-thirds . . . also opposed a mother's being employed while her children were preschoolers."[30]

The flight into femininity that many young women undergo in adolescence is an urgent concern because it leads them to develop personality traits that put them at a disadvantage if and when they attempt to move into traditionally male fields, such as natural science and engineering. If women are to enjoy equality with men in Western societies, they must be socialized in a way that will prepare them for the experiences they will face during adulthood. But because the traditional female role requires noncompetitiveness with men, young women caught in the flight to femininity often experience a decline in school motivations and career aspirations relative to young men; a narrowing of interests;[31] lower self-esteem than young men;[32] less confidence in their academic abilities; and a tendency to blame themselves for failures or shortcomings that are, in fact, beyond their control.[33]

Given that females obtain higher grades throughout primary and secondary school, it is alarming that their interest in things academic drops off later.[34] Moreover, forcing women to conform to the ideals of femininity appears to seriously restrict their repertoire of socially approved behaviors.[35] This "homogenization" of women[36] is crystallized during adolescence when women are taught that they must primarily attend to their appearance and popularity (supposedly to attract the best mate). As noted by Nielsen, research indicates that "adolescent girls base more of their self-esteem on their appearance, their social standing, and on the approval of other people" than men do.[37]

Adolescent females also tend to be more dissatisfied with their appearance than males. Research consistently reveals that most American teenage women dislike their bodies, and many believe that they are overweight, even though they are usually of average or below-average weight. Finally, while teenage boys are also under pressure from arbitrary appearance norms (e.g., to be tall, muscular, and "macho"), it does not appear to be "killing them" in the same way that young women "kill themselves" with the types of obsessive dieting associated with anorexia nervosa and bulimia.[38] As we see below, young men take a more direct route to killing themselves.

How do we explain these gender differences and the intensification of femininity and masculinity? We will illustrate the social processes contributing to the flight to femininity by referring to two of the most important socializing institutions of advanced industrial society: mass education and the mass media.[39]

**Mass education.**   Referring to the impact of schools on females, Paul Chance writes that there "is a large body of research showing how schools at every level teach girls to act helpless [*sic*], sit quietly and find math and science difficult." By adolescence "peer pressure to conform combines with the need to be popular. Suddenly, assertive girls act demure, worried that talent will scare boys away."[40] As we see below, studies continue to reveal that secondary schools are structured, both formally and informally, in a way that undermines the self-confidence of young women, particularly in relation to areas traditionally defined as male, which are ultimately connected to political and economic power. Three factors that affect females' self-confidence are: course streaming, the way teachers respond to them in the classroom, and peer group attitudes.

Course streaming results from a number of subtle and not-so-subtle factors. The more subtle ones include gender stereotyping in textbooks and conversational cues from teachers,[41] while the not-so-subtle factors include the attitudes of guidance counselors, many of whom have stereotyped ideas about women and gender roles. Readers who believe that gender equality has already been achieved will be surprised to know that "gender stereotyping is common among [high school] counsellors . . . and that they often steer female students away from certain college prep courses, particularly in mathematics and the sciences."[42]

Recent research suggests that teachers tend to encourage and publicly praise male students more than girls and are friendlier to them.[43] Teachers also ask males more challenging questions and take time to help them think through principles rather than simply giving them the right answers, as they do for girls.[44] Nielsen notes that these practices are especially evident in mathematics courses and affect young women's estimation of their abilities in this area. In addition, many math teachers believe that females have less of an aptitude for math than males and consequently discourage them from taking this subject seriously. As Nielsen concludes: "Given this state of affairs, it is perhaps not too surprising that girls with the same mathematical abilities as boys tend to underestimate their abilities, while males tend to overestimate theirs."[45]

Similarly, Aletha Huston and Mildred Alvarez conclude on the basis of their extensive review of the relevant literature that during adolescence both males and females are taught to see scientific and computer skills as male domains.[46] Consequently, males develop more confidence about their skills in these areas and practice them more than females do.

Finally, peer attitudes reinforce these biases. As Claire Renzetti and Daniel Curran note, research shows that young women perceived as having masculine traits or who aspire to traditionally masculine fields tend to be considered "undesirable heterosexual partners and friends."[47]

It is little wonder, then, that adolescent women experience a decline in career aspirations and underestimate their academic abilities. Those not planning to go on to college tend to enroll in "home economics, cosmetology, and secretarial programs that prepare them to be homemakers or to take jobs with salaries far lower than the skilled trades that employ mostly men. . . . Even college-bound girls shy away from courses such as those in advanced mathematics and science that will prepare them to pursue further study for the most highly paid and prestigious professions."[48] These trends are still strong among working-class women, but are no longer as strong among middle-class women.[49]

***Mass media.*** When we examine the impact of mass media, we find that many of the same stereotypes and expectations found within the educational system are directed at young people. It is no coincidence that youths in North America are enthusiastic consumers of mass media products, such as magazines, movies, television, advertising, and music. One does not have to examine statistics to conclude that these media are interconnected. For example, "teenzines" (teen magazines directed at young women) report the latest news about fashion and music trends, and they link these with other youth-oriented, leisure industries through advertising. A recent study examined three leading American teenzines published in 1988 and 1989 and found that almost one-half of the total magazine space was taken up by ads (see chart 3.1) and that about one-half of these ads were selling beauty-care products, fashion, clothing, and other items designed to enhance young women's appearance and popularity (see chart 3.2). Only about three percent of these ads were education- or career-oriented.[50]

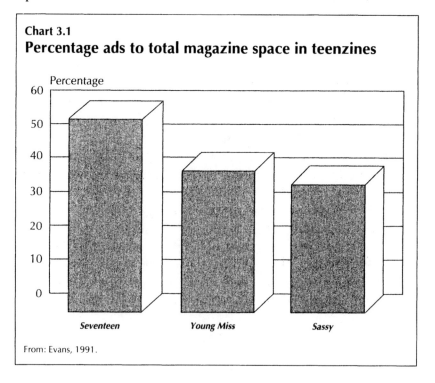

**Chart 3.1**
**Percentage ads to total magazine space in teenzines**

From: Evans, 1991.

In discussing their findings, Ellis Evans and his colleagues note that although the overt theme of these magazines is self-improvement, they covertly suggest that this should be done by conforming to fashion trends and engaging in physical beautification. Articles that deal with political issues and social responsibility are scarce. Instead, the existing articles reinforce the message of the ads that "the road to happiness is attracting males for successful heterosexual life by way of physical beautification." Evans and his co-researchers go on to note the similarity between teenzines and fashion magazines aimed at adult women, which "emphasize interpersonal relations and the value of success through personal attractiveness."[51] We would go one step further and contend that these teenzines contribute to an indoctrination into the "cult of femininity"[52] that has taken hold during this century, partly as a result of the efforts of advertisers.[53] These teenzines have a

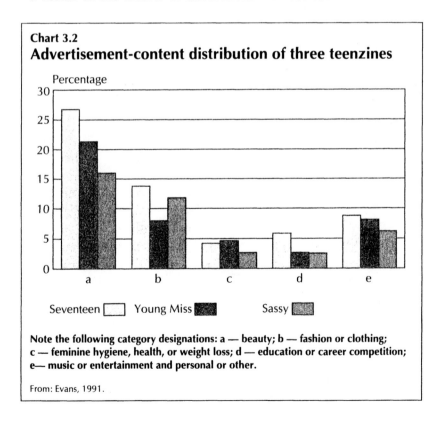

**Chart 3.2**
**Advertisement-content distribution of three teenzines**

Note the following category designations: a — beauty; b — fashion or clothing; c — feminine hygiene, health, or weight loss; d — education or career competition; e— music or entertainment and personal or other.

From: Evans, 1991.

collective circulation of about 2.5 million issues per year, so it is little wonder that women in the United States now spend over one million dollars per hour on cosmetics.[54]

The impact of television is equally deleterious. Young Americans spend three to four hours per day watching TV.[55] By age 18, young Americans see more of the television than the classroom, and by their mid-twenties, watching television is third only to sleep and work as a daily activity.[56] Furthermore, the world of television is also still a male domain, with male characters outnumbering female characters, particularly in more dominant and dynamic roles. As Donald Davis notes, the "television female's existence still seems to be largely a function of her youth and beauty." Women still tend to play roles in which they are "more ornamental . . . than functional" and in which they are portrayed as "young, attractive, and sexy." Davis also found that in TV programs women are still "much more *defined* in their roles where men are much more indeterminate."[57]

Research investigating the impact of television has found that its sexism is transmitted to young people. For example, the amount of television viewed by men and women has been connected with sexist attitudes and a greater endorsement of traditional gender-role division of household chores.[58] Again, television conveys the message that young women should strive to be "feminine" and adopt traditional roles. Interestingly, research has also found that sexist attitudes can be reversed through "counterstereotyped portrayals of women" in television programs,[59] but such portrayals are rarely presented on network television or in popular film.

More disturbing is the influence that rock videos have on young people's attitudes toward sex. These videos are telecast continually on MTV, a channel specifically targeted at young people. Research has shown that heavy viewers of MTV more readily accept sexual violence. Huston and Alvarez found that "the more females watch MTV, the more likely they are to believe that men are violent toward women, that violence is part of love and sex, and that women cannot or should not defend themselves from male aggression."[60] Given the current concerns about acquaintance rape and sexual assault, it is curious that there is not more concern about this type of programming.

How do young men fare in the gender intensification process? Research indicates that males are conditioned to believe that they "are more valuable, competent, and powerful than females."[61] But, of course, this statement must be considered in the context of other things we have looked at in this book. For example, in chapter 1 we saw that young men are neither as highly paid nor as gainfully employed as adults and that they have the second highest suicide rate of all age/gender groups.

As we have argued, a flight into masculinity is also part of the identity manipulation and economic exploitation of young men. The stereotypes regarding what it means to be a man are everywhere: in the schools, the media, and peer groups. Advertisers sell clothing, music, beer, and cigarettes with the cliché of the tough, aloof, macho male. While there are few mass-circulation magazines that target only teenage males, publications aimed at adult men, which young men read, "focus on themes of sexuality (*Playboy*), sports (*Field and Stream*), and daring (*Road and Track*)."[62] In high schools, the emphasis on athletic excellence reinforces the macho stereotype.[63]

With all the talk these days of the "new man" who has supposedly emerged in conjunction with the women's movement, many men who display sensitivity and warmth — their so-called feminine side — complain that the women in their lives actually shun them for more traditional males. This is because they have been conditioned to find the macho stereotype sexually attractive."[64] Young men who do not conform to these macho roles perpetuated by the media are stigmatized. As Marie Richmond-Abbott argues, the "penalty for not living up to the norms of being tough, being 'cool,' and being good is severe: rejection or simply being ignored."[65] And, of course, most males are not suited to such a role, either intellectually or temperamentally. Yet there are few alternatives available for "sensitive misfits,"[66] so that those who attempt to formulate an identity that is less conventionally masculine face a formidable task.

Nielsen summarizes the stereotype young men must contend with when trying to come of age in American society:

Males are . . . held hostage to their gender role in that masculinity is equated with being bigger, taller, and more muscular than other males — and certainly bigger, taller, and bulkier than females. Indeed, the research consistently shows that we tend to ascribe more masculine personality traits to males who fit our stereotypical image of the tall, muscular he-man. Without knowing him, we expect the mesomorph (lean, muscular) to be more independent, competitive, self-confident, active, daring, and invulnerable than the male with a smaller, slighter build.[67]

Obviously, most males cannot live up to this stereotype, yet many feel compelled to try to do so, as a result of the conditioning to which they have been subjected. The attempt to fulfill this image is linked by researchers to the "high death rates from murder, drunk driving, and stress-related illnesses" among young men.[68] Males are also under pressure to be popular and to pursue women, but contradictions in these pressures lead them to feel alienated from their peers and from the women whose company they seek.[69] Macho stereotypes also divert many young men who might otherwise be inclined to take up careers that are not traditionally male-dominated. Stereotypes also truncate emotional development by making young men feel they should not express their weaknesses and vulnerabilities (research shows that men who do so are not well liked) and that they should not cry or seek help. As a result, some young men end up harming "themselves physically and psychologically."[70] Trying to formulate a viable and stable identity when social pressures contradict one's internal needs and capacities can be very difficult.

Warren Farrell has caricatured the negative aspects of the male gender role that are perpetuated by the ideology of gender in the following "ten commandments of masculinity":

1. Thou shalt not cry or in other ways display fear, weakness, sympathy, empathy, or involvement before thy neighbour.

2. Thou shalt not be vulnerable but shalt honor and respect the "logical," "practical," or "intellectual" — as thou definest them.

3. Thou shalt not listen for the sake of listening — it is a waste of time.

4. Thou shalt not commit introspection.

5. Thou shalt be condescending to women in every way.

6. Thou shalt control thy wife's body and all its relations.

7. Thou shalt have no other breadwinners before thee.

8. Thou shalt not be responsible for housework or childcare.

9. Thou shalt honor and obey the straight and narrow path to success: Job specialization.

10. Thou shalt have an answer to all problems at all times.[71]

## COMING OF AGE IN THE WAKE OF GENDER INTENSIFICATION

Since we have just argued that most adolescents are pressured and conditioned to accept exaggerated conceptions of their femininity and masculinity, it is appropriate to consider the long-term impact of gender intensification on them as they make their way into adulthood. Accordingly, we will now examine the issue of how young women and men come of age and develop an adult identity after experiencing prolonged identity manipulation in the form of gender conditioning.

Relative to their female peers, young males appear to experience more of a continuity in their coming of age. In general, the orientations and values they learn during childhood and adolescence correspond to those they are expected to assume as adults. Most males anticipate occupying work and career roles. Moreover, most do not experience a conflict between their career plans and plans to marry and start a family: the latter would not jeopardize the former.[72] The industrial capitalist workplace has been based on the assumption that free household labor, in the form of a wife, is available to wage earners.[73] Many young men assume that this scenario is still the norm, in spite of dramatic increases in the number of women in the workplace, a phenomenon that can perhaps be explained by stereotyped portrayals of women in the media.[74]

Despite the fact that many men are prepared to assume just one main role, that of the breadwinner, their lot is not always an easy one. For example, since fewer women are willing to play the role of the traditional housewife, many men have to adjust their expectations as they move into adulthood. In addition, research has amply documented the widespread identity crises among the contemporary American and Canadian male associated with discrepancies between occupational choice and belief systems.[75] However, young men have an advantage in the sense that their preparation for adulthood is less inappropriate than is that of young women.

Young women not only face confusing and contradictory sets of roles and values, but many are also exposed to influences during adolescence that set them on a course of development that is often not continued during adulthood. As we have stressed, young women are conditioned to concentrate on their appearance and popularity and are steered away from the type of courses and activities that would prepare them for adult life in the contemporary workplace. Indeed, research reveals that many young women pass through adolescence and young adulthood with little awareness of the political and economic workings of their society, with few firm career plans and an assumption that they will marry, start a family, and "live happily ever after."[76] These expectations might have been realistic in previous generations, but changes in the economy, the workplace, and contemporary life-styles mean that an increasing number of women will not marry at all, or that they will marry much later. Canadian estimates are that one in seven women will never marry (double the figure from 20 years ago), and those who do are waiting until age 26 on average.[77] Those who do marry often face the prospect of having to work to contribute to the family income while at the same time doing most of the child-rearing and domestic work. Only one out of three married women in Canada currently remains a full-time homemaker.[78] Many also experience separation and single motherhood, with its attendant high rate of poverty.[79] Thus, women are increasingly finding that the "live happily ever after" part of the traditional script does not come true. Rather, their situation can lead to economic deprivation and psychological turmoil unless precautions are taken.

Research on ego identity formation provides further evidence of the emotional turmoil that contemporary women can experience. For example, women often experience an identity crisis later than men. While men may have a crisis in their late teens and early 20s, women are more likely to undergo one in their late 20s or their 30s. Such a crisis often takes place after they have attempted to follow a traditional or "semitraditional" life-style.[80] The gender intensification that occurs during adolescence appears to convince many young women that their attractiveness is the asset upon which they should base their adult identity. Unfortunately, feminine beauty, as it is defined in Western culture, diminishes with age. Gloria Steinem has remarked that many young women shun feminism and opt for traditional sources of status because they are enticed by the rewards the system gives them. This strategy often proves to be ill-advised in the long run, and if the lower status associated with marriage and childbearing does not diminish their social and interpersonal power, age eventually does. The aging process can precipitate a prolonged identity crisis, often accompanied by anger and frustration.

Changing one's identity during adulthood can be extremely difficult and painful, and women who do so must contend with a workplace that offers them low status and low-paying jobs, or alternatively they face a long educational process, which may not result in a job in their area of expertise (see the underemployment statistics presented in chart 2.1). In many Western countries, women are concentrated in clerical, service, and sales jobs, all of which are low in status and pay less than most of the other male-dominated jobs. In Canada and the United States, women working full-time consistently make between 60 and 70 percent of what males make, sometimes even within specific job categories.[81] These figures indicate that socialization is not the only factor holding adult women back; rather, salary discrimination becomes an issue.

To return to the gender-intensification argument, many women are conditioned during adolescence not to aspire to jobs traditionally held by men and often limit their career prospects early on by not pursing the educational prerequisites for certain positions. In the current highly competitive, recession-plagued job market, securing a good job is difficult for everyone, even if one begins early in the conventional career stream. While programs now exist to train or retrain women, these are scarce in many countries, opportunities are limited, and the change of identity required to become a professional or a tradesperson can be daunting.

Women who do enter the workplace often find themselves in a competitive world, where they are not always welcome or well treated. Having been socialized to be empathetic and relationship-oriented, they now must contend with men who have been conditioned to be competitive and more egocentric. Some males are especially tough with females whom they see as rivals for scarce jobs and resources. Women can have difficulty acclimatizing themselves to the cold office environment and often discover that their possibilities for career advancement are limited because of the "glass ceiling" created by gender discrimination and the tight job market.

More women are becoming aware of these problems and are turning to feminism for answers to them. Feminism holds out a potential for liberation and can furnish women with interpersonal support systems. However, without the endorsement of the rest of society, it cannot work as a viable alternative to more traditional views of what it means to be a woman. Moreover, the competing camps within the feminist movement can confuse those searching for a new identity.

These internal divisions become apparent when one looks at the three types of feminism discussed in current university textbooks that deal with gender roles. *Liberal feminism* advocates work within the system to address gender inequalities; this approach is now often dismissed as too conservative, mainstream, and middle-class.[82] On the other hand, *socialist feminism* identifies capitalism and patriarchy as the source of gender inequalities and calls for a revolution to liberate women. Finally, *radical feminism*, the most vocal branch of the movement in many universities today, "considers women's oppression to be *the* fundamental oppression."[83] Within radical feminism there are several subgroups, including lesbian feminism and cultural feminism. The former affirms that "lesbianism is the only acceptable sexual expression for women,"[84] and that "only lesbians . . . can fight sexism fully, since heterosexual women's attachments to men keep them from breaking free of male opinion and power."[85] Another of its tenets is that equality can be achieved through "grassroots organizations, confrontational politics, and by building an alternative culture."[86] Cultural feminism emphasizes innate differences between men and women with "'women's' qualities of nurturance, caring, cooperativeness, and nonviolence . . . viewed as superior to 'men's' qualities."[87]

In spite of its lack of internal coherence, feminism is becoming more institutionalized in universities and more women are turning to it as an avenue through which they can find themselves and develop a voice with which to express their dissent.

The key to identity manipulation lies in Erikson's concept of the psychosocial. That is, to manipulate an identity the object is first to make the psyche vulnerable and tenuous. Then the vulnerable psyche is manipulated socially — its needs for acceptance, community, self-definition, and a sense of purpose in life are exploited. With sources for the gratification of these needs removed, other sources have been put into place, many of which serve the interests of others. In the case of adolescents and young adults, this has been accomplished in advanced industrial society through the establishment and legitimation of the institutions and practices associated with the identity moratorium. We believe that few escape the reaches of this identity manipulation, and that this principle applies to both females and males, as well as to all racial and ethnic groups and social classes. However, affluent and privileged youths are less adversely affected by it than those who are less fortunate.

# Part Two

**The Political Economy of Youth**

*The political economy view of youth focuses on the concepts of the manufacture of consent, ideology, and complementarity.*

▶ *Chapter 4 defines the concept of ideology and applies it to the attempt to create social stability with a) a language that defines the parameters of appropriate behavior among young people and b) institutions that enforce the definitions embodied in the language (e.g., the educational system). Thus, we show how collective constructions of reality constitute a form of social control — measures initiated to maintain order and continuity in a society through the manufacture of consent. We also note that the attempt to manufacture consent has given rise to a certain amount of dissent.*

▶ *The themes of ideology and social order are explored further in chapter 5, which introduces the concept of complementarity and applies it to techniques of manipulation and social control in the manufacture of consent. The principle of complementarity is illustrated with youth in the service economy and the roles played by various social institutions (education, advertising, the media) in preparing young people for their future roles as disciplined, low-waged producers and easily manipulated consumers.*

103

▶ *The concluding chapter of this book looks at Sweden as a possible alternative to the Canadian–American model of coming of age. Though Sweden's social institutions are by no means perfect, the country's history of experimentation with progressive social policies has enabled it to respond more favorably to youths and reduce the degree of their disenfranchisement. By examining employment levels, wage rates, job opportunities, and life chances created by the Swedish government, we demonstrate how coming of age today can be a positive experience for the young. Using the Swedish example, we show how the integration of youthful and adult activities can enrich adult society. By way of conclusion, we offer some other suggestions about how to deal with the problems facing young North Americans as they come of age.*

▶ *The second part of this book uses a more innovative approach than the first. Here we add a literary dimension to our argument by comparing the experience Western youths have when coming of age today with the dystopias envisioned by George* Orwell *in* Nineteen Eighty-Four *and Aldous Huxley in* Brave New World.

# 4

---

# Ideology and the Politics of Social Control

---

## THE MANUFACTURE OF CONSENT

The term *manufacturing consent* was coined by the journalist Walter Lippmann and has subsequently been used by Edward Herman and Noam Chomsky,[1] as well as Helen Caldicott.[2] Herman and Chomsky use the concept to show how the mass media filter information so that the interests of political, military, and economic elites go unchallenged. Caldicott employs the concept in her description of how American business interests spread antiunionism and a fear of communism by using public relations techniques, while at the same time equating free enterprise with democracy and God. Caldicott argues that it became necessary to manufacture public consensus in the United States after the right to vote was extended to those who did not own property (during the 19th century). By the 1920s, everyone over 21 years of age in Canada and the United States could vote. Dominant economic and political elites realized that because the general public could then influence public policy, they had to take measures to ensure that the public voted in favor of policies that were in the interests of the elites. Hence, they created waves of public relations campaigns to entrench certain beliefs among the general public.

The title of Edward Bernays's book *The Engineering of Consent* echoes Lippmann's coinage.[3] The book unabashedly catalogs persuasion techniques developed by public relations firms. Bernays himself pioneered many of the techniques that are still in use, and his book was a standard text in the public relations industry for years. When one reads his book, it becomes clear how mass consent could be engineered by "adjustment" of public opinion. The author's alleged bragging about how he "taught" women to smoke cigarettes through his advertising campaigns underlines his insensitivity to the implications of his dubious techniques.[4]

In all of the preceding contexts, the manufacture of consent refers to the way in which dominant institutions insidiously shape public opinion. Writers such as Chomsky and Caldicott charge that corporations, the media, the educational system, and other institutions that are responsible for informing the public are actually engaged in campaigns of persuasion designed to engineer their consent. If we were talking about China or the former Soviet Union, for example, we would more readily be expected to call these practices propaganda campaigns because they supposedly involve misinformation and manipulation. But whether we use the term *persuasion* or *propaganda*, the result is the same: what passes as a freely arrived at consensus is often a set of fictions that have been fabricated by mercenary image-makers. Thus, the social and economic order that is said to characterize advanced industrial societies is painted by writers such as Chomsky and Herman as quite superficial and illusory.

However, when the illusion of order gives way to the reality of control, and when the disgruntlement and alienation previously kept beneath the surface begin to erupt, a chaotic social situation can result. In the case of youth in contemporary Western societies, a tremendous amount of dissent has been building, which has now risen to the surface and is being manifested through crime and violence. The increasing need for armed guards in some high schools, the spread of warring youth gangs in suburban neighborhoods, and a growing sense of fatalism and aimlessness are all signs of this discontent. Attempts to manufacture consent among an alienated and disenfranchised group have clearly backfired and are manufacturing a climate of youth dissent.

In spite of the impossibility of producing absolute conformity, the manufacture of consent remains politically expedient for those who occupy the commanding heights of the leading economic, political, and social institution. This is because, in order to preserve their positions of privilege, they must convince the nonprivileged that their place at the bottom of the social hierarchy is justified and that they have only themselves to blame for their low status. This is done by nurturing the belief that in democratic societies both failure and success are individually accomplished. Without this belief, the potential for social disruption emerges because the disenfranchised can understand their problems in systemic rather than in individual terms. The manufacturing of consent must therefore be an ongoing concern for those in positions of authority. Moreover, manufacturing consent is critical in an era when concerns intensify that cheap labor in Third World countries threatens jobs in North America (as in the case of NAFTA), and when youth are emerging as the economic equivalents of cheap, Third World workers in the central service sectors of the advanced economies.

## THE IDEOLOGY OF YOUTH

In our investigation of how coming of age is experienced and structured in advanced industrial societies, we encountered a number of commonsense beliefs about the process. The average person looks upon adolescence as a natural and necessary stage of development and feels that this period is the time of one's life when one is carefree and has no responsibilities.

People often assume that the way the young are regulated is in their best interest and that they should therefore eagerly accept it. This regulation is thought to be necessary because young people are seen as functioning in a reduced capacity due to their biological immaturity. Many accept these widespread beliefs. It can be argued, however, that they actually make life more difficult for young people because they are based on stereotypes that deny them basic respect as individuals in their own right. These stereotyped views are based on a kind of loopy logic that makes it difficult for young people to escape the prejudices directed at them: since young people appear to be acting immaturely, it is presumed that they are inherently or biologically incapable of doing otherwise. Their apparent inability to assume responsibility leads one to think that only close adult supervision and monitoring could ensure their proper functioning in society.

Many young people do not, or cannot, accept such narrow conceptions of what they *should* be like, particularly when these conceptions deny essential parts of their character. Moreover, when they openly reject the conditions imposed on them during adolescence, others believe there must be something wrong with them that makes them unable to control themselves. Not surprisingly, if one denies individuals experiences involving mature and responsible roles, they will likely remain immature and irresponsible.

We believe it is unreasonable to expect individuals to learn the requirements of maturity and responsibility without allowing them to perform roles in which maturity and responsibility are exercised. Maturity and responsibility are qualities that are acquired through experience and practice. They cannot be gained by reading textbooks or through classroom instruction alone. We believe that until we understand this, many of the problems people associate with youths and blame on them will continue.

But where did this negative view of youth come from? As we saw, youth was "discovered" by social scientists early in this century when young people appeared to pose a problem for industrial society. This discovery gave birth to an ideology of youth that has contributed to a consensus about the "true" nature of this period of life. Interestingly, this scientific ideology coincides with the commonsense view of youth and it serves the dominant economic interests in Western societies. As such, it is encouraged and supported by these dominant interests, which have exploited social scientific theories about youth to further their own ends. For example, the ideology of youth helps justify using young people as a source of cheap labor. At the very least, dominant interests simply had to heed the words of Huxley, who affirmed in *Brave New World* that in order for the status quo to be maintained and the established system to run smoothly the disenfranchised must be made to love their servitude or at least not to recognize it as servitude.

To understand the ideology of youth we must begin with the fundamental question of politics which, in the present context, speaks simply to the distribution of power in society. Young people, as we have argued, lack power, rights, and legitimacy, which means they are disenfranchised. At the same time, however, they are crucial to the economic system because they constitute a source of cheap labor, as well as a massive consumer market. Politically and economically speaking, then, those in control have to ensure that young people do not realize the extent to which they are crucial to the survival of the system. And they must also ensure that they do not band together and rebel against the system. To prevent this kind of uprising and maintain the status quo, dominant interests use ideology and subtle ideological control.

An ideology comprises a body of systematic beliefs and ideas that function simultaneously to magnify certain aspects of social reality and to mask others. For example, the ideology of Christianity is based on the belief that Christians are kind, that they do good works, try to save souls, and are opposed to all forms of injustice. While this may be true, it masks the fact that as a Christian organization the Catholic church is sexist. It was racist for its past ownership of slaves and continues to be complicit in exploitative colonialist and imperialist ventures around the world.

As another example, we may consider democracy. The ideology of democracy involves a political philosophy that encourages the pursuit of individual liberty, social equality, freedom from tyranny, and self-determination of all peoples. This is true at one level, but like the ideology of Christianity, it masks its support of dictators in the Third World. It also blinds its adherents to the unjust wars waged abroad in the name of democracy, and to the racism, sexism, poverty, ghettos, and social inequality that exist at home.

Those who promote the ideologies of Christianity and democracy have at their disposal very efficient tools of mass social control. With great success, they are able to secure complete loyalty to their cause, for the ideologies of Christianity and democracy are uncritically accepted by hundreds of millions of people around the world in their daily sacred and secular lives. They are prepared to go to war in support of these ideologies and to sanction huge expenditures to defend them.

The fervor with which an ideology is embraced, particularly its persistence in light of its unsavory aspects, leads us to consider another of its features. The earlier statement that ideology is a body of systematic beliefs and ideas should be modified to stress that it is primarily a body of beliefs and only secondarily a body of ideas. The distinction is more than just semantic, though, for while ideas are generally open to scientific testing, validation, and verification, beliefs are not.[5] As systems of beliefs, ideologies are difficult to evaluate on empirical grounds.

While capable of exerting a tremendous influence on peoples' perceptions and behavior, then, ideologies are not strictly subject to verification. This invites us to consider the relationship between ideology and science, or ideology and truth. Ideologies are like dogmas. Their adherents say they embody truths but do not propose a method to substantiate such claims. In contrast, scientific principles and evidence can be questioned, tested, refuted, or upheld. The scientist agrees to debate publicly his or her theories and to let others play a role in determining whether there is any relationship between the ideas and "facticity." As Gustav Bergmann suggests, an ideological statement is "a value judgement disguised as, or mistaken for, a statement of fact."[6] Garvin McCain and Erwin Segal are equally suspicious of ideology and equate it with dogma: "One way of contrasting science and dogma is to say that a scientist accepts facts as given and belief systems as tentative, whereas a dogmatist accepts the belief systems as given; facts are irrelevant."[7]

In sum, an ideology is a system of beliefs, which claims to represent the truth but is not open to empirical verification. To become accessible to the masses it is important to ensure the ideological simplification of truth and reality through the use of symbols, images, appeals to emotion, socially accepted values, and high-sounding moral principles. In all of this, the role of language is of paramount importance.

## LANGUAGE AND IDEOLOGY

Language is essential in structuring the perception of reality. Without language, the ability to think in complex terms is undermined. Even thinking about concrete, immediate objects and events is difficult unless one first has a name for these things. Language provides us with complex sets of names or symbols, and it is with these symbols that we communicate to others how we perceive reality.

As noted earlier, a particular language was developed that disparages adolescents, and this language also served to delegitimize them and depict them as marginal to what is positively valued in society. Adolescence and youth are seen as a period in life when raging hormones turn hitherto well-behaved children into unmanageable tyrants. As we have seen, this view is especially prevalent among those who subscribe to the psychiatric model of development, which now has a technical language that belittles young people.

It is essential to our analysis that we examine the ideological aspects of language and how language is used to control youth for political ends. Where this kind of control is most effective is in its ability to manipulate people openly, while at the same time making those same people see the control as beneficial to the society at large.

From the perspective of a capitalist economy based on liberal democracy where citizens are endowed with many freedoms and rights, and where any overt economic or political coercion would be inappropriate, the language of order and control are indispensable. In this case, language is charged with defining coercion in acceptable ways — with portraying exploitation in benign terms. This is the power of ideology. It can mask certain aspects of a given situation while magnifying other aspects. An example can be seen in the name Canadians give the Ministry of War: Department of National Defence. The main idea is that we are never the aggressors; instead, we are always reacting to aggression and defending ourselves nobly. One cannot conceive of this ministry being called the Department of National Offence, can one? If exploitation is presented in benevolent terms as "giving one an economic break," and if workers accept this, then they are far less likely to rise up against the "benevolent" employer and demand such things as higher wages, better labor agreements, more benefits, healthier working conditions, and so on.

What we have been discussing is the political sociology of language. But what exactly is this school of sociology? And why is it integral to the politics of social order and social control? To answer these questions we need to stand back and contemplate the large picture.

## THE MACROPOLITICAL CONTEXT

Before the era of glasnost in the former Soviet Union and the end of the Cold War, many Soviet people lived in a black-and-white world. One was either with the regime or against it; one was either part of the solution or part of the problem. Those who inhabited the free world either pitied the less fortunate who lived behind the Iron Curtain or condemned them as sinister inhabitants of an "evil empire."

With the dismantling of socialism in the former Soviet Bloc, the Communist threat appears to have evaporated. But now demons have now been created out of old allies (Manuel Noriega in Panama and Saddam Hussein in Iraq), and old demons have become new allies (Mikhail Gorbachev in Russia and Hafez Al Assad in Syria). Secret deals have even been made all along with the enemy of enemies — Iran, which was an ally in the West's war with Iraq. The Iran-contra scandal revealed that Iran also played a crucial (though covert) role in support of the American administration's undeclared war against Nicaragua in the 1980s. In addition, it is alleged that Iran agreed to assist the Reagan election campaign against outgoing Democratic President Jimmy Carter by delaying the release of American hostages held in Iran.

During the 1980s, then, Iran was the enemy with whom the West made secret deals and against whom the West supported Iraq. Now, in the 1990s, the hostages are free, Nicaragua is again a friendly ally, Iraq is the enemy, and the status of Iran in Western eyes is still dubious. If all this sounds like double-talk and "newspeak," that is because it is! As a technique of social control it was very effectively employed in George Orwell's fictitious society of Oceania in *Nineteen Eighty-Four*. In his society, the government of Big Brother constantly manipulated the population by playing with words, inverting their meanings, and rewriting history to suit its own interests. A parallel phenomenon is occurring in contemporary Western society: today's freedom-fighters are yesterday's terrorists; the "evil empire" is now receiving billions of dollars in aid from the West, although the West previously spent billions trying to ruin that empire.

For some, this might appear confusing and contradictory; to others, it is eminently reasonable and sensible. This duplicity attests to the power of language which, when used for political ends, can dramatically alter the way reality is perceived. The United States and its allies constitute the free world, while the socialist countries (Cuba, China, North Korea, and so on) make up the unfree world. Of course these words are labels; but such labels are important since they represent the filters through which we see the world. That Westerners view their political and economic trading partners as their friends and those of the socialists as their puppets reveals the extent to which our everyday language, or labels, define ways of seeing.[8] And, the ways in which we see things determines how we act.

In understanding these matters it is necessary to be sensitive to the complex relationship between ways of seeing the world and ways of acting in the free world. Westerners claim to know very well what those in the unfree world do and what they are like. But this so-called knowledge is clearly ideological. What many citizens of the free world do not know, and what they are not encouraged to examine critically, is what they themselves do and what they are like. In other words, if one accepts that the West's perception of others is ideological, one might also expect that the West's perception of itself is ideological.

Whether we deal with the West as a whole or with an individual country in the West, one thing is certain — neither is a homogeneous entity. Within each country, economic, political, and social interest groups abound, and each of these groups attempts to influence its citizens. It is in this context that we examine the categories of youth and adolescence with a view to assessing the degrees to which various public and private institutions and agencies in the free world control, cajole, and manipulate fellow citizens without their knowledge. Even in those cases where dominant interests seem to be acting for the public good, one has to separate the immediate consequences of their actions from the long-term ones. For example, when governments create temporary youth employment initiatives, such as summer job-training programs, the immediate beneficiary may be the young person looking for a job. However, in the end, the major benefit often accrues to the employer, who acquires a person trained at public expense, in effect, someone who is able to work efficiently and thus be exploited more.[9]

Discussing the callous manipulation of young people is admittedly a radical way of bringing to light the process by which control is effected. However, it is necessary because Westerners are all too quick to point to other countries for examples of controlled populations, and refuse to entertain the fact that they are also subject to control. This explains why they see themselves as free. They equate freedom with the absence of control, particularly physical control; and it is on this basis that Soviet citizens, for example, were traditionally seen as "unfree."

## IDEOLOGY AND ILLUSION

Politically, it has always been convenient for those who occupy the commanding heights of Western economic and political institutions to be able to distract the disenfranchised citizenry from the reality of their own exploitation by pointing to the sad fate of the hapless prisoners of socialist society. Hence by comparison, the lowest-paid workers, the unemployed, the underemployed, and all other manner of disenfranchised groups in the West are made to feel better about their lowly positions in their own societies. For though they may not be able to boast the material trappings of success, they are convinced that theirs is a free society; that they as individuals are free; and that they could acquire the trappings of success if they really tried hard enough.

The meaning of their own poverty and low status escapes them, as do the realities of systemic racism and sexism that affect natives living on reserves, racial or ethnic minorities living in ghettoes, and others. Both the victims of these social evils and the more fortunate are conditioned to believe that the victims must be personally responsible for their plight. For along with the personal freedoms afforded by the free society, there also come personal responsibilities. In socialist countries, on the other hand, any social malaise is automatically attributed by Westerners to shortcomings of the socialist system itself. The ideological implication is that while individuals may fall through the cracks in the capitalist, liberal-democratic system, problems in socialist society indicate that the entire socialist system and philosophy are flawed.

This is not meant as an apology for the socialist countries and others where citizens are subject to extreme forms of control. Rather, it is intended to alert those who live in the West of the fact that they are not immune from more insidious types of manipulation. Furthermore, in most of the nonsocialist, totalitarian countries where social control is not so subtle, and where human rights are violated daily, we must acknowledge the fact that the West often puts the tyrants in power and keeps them there. Saddam Hussein and Manuel Noreiga are merely the most recent examples of this phenomenon.

Within the Western countries themselves, however, the young are not the only group that suffers. It is equally possible to trace the means by which women, racial and ethnic minorities, and workers are targeted for control and manipulation, often without their even realizing it. Again, their oppression can be ascribed to the power of language and the ability of those who use it for political ends to define reality in ways that are consistent with their own interests.

The use of language is ideological in that it conceals more than it reveals. It masks key aspects of social reality that need to be closely analyzed. Such an analysis could serve to disrupt the social order that is built on the West's supposedly superior morals and call into question the very legitimacy on which the system is founded. Our own critical study is an attempt to expose the way in which entrenched interests manipulate people, in particular the young.

## THE POLITICS OF SOCIAL CONTROL

Since those who exploit the young can profit from their actions, it is understandable why they are interested in keeping them in the dark. The key concern is with control at both the physical and the ideological levels. The instruments and techniques of physical control are widely recognized: police, courts, prisons, asylums, armies, and so on. As we have mentioned, though, the more insidious techniques of ideological control that are used very effectively to manipulate people are not so widely recognized and need further explanation.

Broadly speaking social control can have one of two consequences. It can either deny groups and individuals liberty, or promote liberty. But far from being an all-or-nothing phenomenon, control and freedom are matters of degree. Moreover, they are not mutually exclusive and contradictory phenomena, for clearly some degree of control is indispensable to both individual and collective freedom. The central questions, therefore, are control by whom? And freedom for whom?

These are questions of power and social class, for the dominant class in any society is advantageously placed to exact obedience or compliance from the subordinate classes. The observation by Karl Marx and Friedrich Engels that "the ideas of the ruling class are in every epoch the ruling ideas" is usually taken as these authors' definitive statement on ideology. Among other things, it implies a relationship not simply between class and ideology, but also between power and ideology — the organized and structured power of a given class: ". . . the class which is the ruling material force of society is at the same time its ruling intellectual force. The class which has the means of material production at its disposal, has control at the same time over the means of mental production."[10]

It is clear, then, that any discussion of ideology also involves considerations of social control. As an instrument of control, the latter is far more efficient and less costly than physical coercion, although it cannot totally replace the use of force, as was seen in the case of the massacre of students at Kent State University by National Guard troops in 1970 (see Mostafa Rejac's essay listed in endnote 5 for this chapter). Not only does this form of control obviate the need for rigid and all-pervasive supervision, it also contributes to social and political stability. If a specific segment of the population, such as youths, can be made by another to pursue actions that run counter to its own interests without perceiving those actions as harmful to itself, then there is no need to embark upon an elaborate program of interventionary control aimed at that segment. This is the sense in which some political economists speak about false consciousness in a subordinate population as one of the surest means by which a dominant class or group can guarantee its continued dominance over the former.

For example, the racist and fascist elements of certain working-class youth gangs serve the purpose of fracturing potential unity among working-class youth as a whole. They also limit the potential effectiveness that youths could have as a bloc if they were to demand decent jobs and housing, relevant educational and training programs, social justice, responsible government, and so on. Because they lack all of these things, working-class youths feel alienated and powerless. As their frustrations mount, they react in two contradictory ways: a) they seek to acquire the material trappings of success defined as acceptable by the ruling class, resorting to crime to obtain these things; and b) they attempt to reject the system altogether by creating a counterculture of drugs, sex, crime, and violence that makes the establishment sit up and take notice.

The divisions that ultimately spring up between the different elements of working-class youth recall the situation described by Frantz Fanon in *The Wretched of the Earth*, where he discussed blacks turning against blacks in the colonial context. He attributes this to the extreme frustration experienced by the colonized person who cannot easily strike out at the colonial master and instead lashes about at his colonized brothers and sisters: "The colonized man will first manifest this aggressiveness which has been deposited in his bones against his own people. This is the period when the niggers beat each other up, and the police and magistrates do not know which way to turn. . . ."[11]

In both Europe and North America, one can find separate youth gangs of working-class white, black, and Jewish skinheads. In Los Angeles Hispanic and black gangs such as Los Diablos and the Bloods brutally attack each other. At the same time, there are also divisions among black youths. Vicious fights periodically break out between the Bloods and Crips, two warring black gangs.[12] A more recent addition to the scene are the equally violent Asian-American youth gangs.

While the young members of these gangs fight it out with each other, both on the streets and in prisons, the main problem goes unnoticed: the failure of the larger social system, and those who benefit from the status quo, to acknowledge their part in the manufacture of dissent and to do something about it. The dominant ideologies of racism and individualism serve to divide working-class youth so that they become blind to their shared interests as a group and fail to realize that they are being oppressed. At the same time, they embrace the values of their oppressors, such as competition and consumerism. As a result, capitalist enterprises are able to sell more hip-hop and designer clothes, jewelry, running shoes, haircuts, movies and videos, compact discs, alcohol, and tobacco, each product being tailored to a different age or ethnic group of the youth population.

We can see just how aggressively business interests exploit young people if we look at business-oriented publications. According to Lawrence Graham and Lawrence Hamdan, in the United States young people are worth $200 billion per year to those in the food, clothing, and music industries. The title of their book *Youthtrends: Capturing the $200 Billion Youth Market*,[13] suggests that the goal of these industries is to finagle this money away from young people in whatever way possible. Those in the business world often have few moral misgivings about the health and well-being of their targeted market. In Canada, marketing researchers estimate that teenagers spend $6 billion per year on consumer products. In a recent issue of *Marketing*, Jo Marney reports that this "spending skews heavily toward style and recreation. Clothing, sporting goods (especially shoes), beauty products, electronics equipment and fast foods top the list of teen spending preferences."[14]

In summing up, it would appear that business interests have no scruples about exploiting young people and taking advantage of the internal divisions within this group. Their marketing strategies result in the young attacking and killing one another for things. But no one really holds the manufacturers and advertisers culpable. The latter escape unscathed with their legitimacy and profits largely intact, and with their potential opponents divided and distracted. One thing is certain, though, from the political-economic perspective: the destructive behavior exhibited by youths today is largely a product of social structure, and the attempt to portray it as biologically determined is ideological.

## THE IDEOLOGY OF YOUTH AND MASS EDUCATION

The ideology of youth owes much to the education system which, in effect, is the official institution governing contemporary youth and adolescence. Indeed, the rise of the ideology of youth can most clearly be illustrated through a historical analysis of the mass educational system, which shows that the system was developed to suit the interests of dominant economic and social groups. These groups discouraged developments that went counter to their aims.

In this analysis, we highlight the ways in which schools currently contain, shape, and condition young people, preparing them to be passive and uncritical workers. These characteristics are suitable for many of the jobs available in advanced industrial societies. The general public tends to accept the idea of mass education as inevitable and necessary, but such a view clearly plays into the hands of those in control; for if mass indoctrination and mass processing can pass for education, then those in positions of authority will encounter no challenge to their rule.

Our guide is Randall Collins's *The Credential Society*,[15] which takes the United States as its model. This ought not to pose a problem, however, since the American system, though different from educational systems in other Western countries in certain details, can be deemed representative as far as basic educational trends and influences are concerned.

Western societies have undeniably become societies in which most occupational roles require credentials formally granted by specially designated bureaucracies. It is no longer considered appropriate for workers to acquire their qualifications and skills in the workplace, except in the case of certain apprenticeships. This mass educational movement was prompted by the social disorganization associated with the Industrial Revolution when primary schools were imposed on the population to instill "moral character."[16] As we shall see, this movement has continued into the present where universities and community colleges hold the monopoly in the accreditation of professional "potential."

Collins notes that apprenticeships were the norm in most trades and professions before the rise of the mass educational system. A comprehensive, age-graded system as we now know it simply did not exist. In fact, formal schooling was not considered important until the 1850s. It was only then that a university education became necessary for the major professions and that high-school degrees were viewed as prerequisites for business and teaching careers. Finally, it was not until the 1920s that the "professions had established firm requirements of higher education, and high school degrees began to become the criterion for clerical work."[17]

While it is well-known that primary schools developed on a mass scale in the 19th century, the widespread resistance to their implementation seems to have been forgotten.[18] By mid-century, laws requiring attendance were emerging, often as part of "moral crusades."[19] The moral crusades were a response to the apparent increase in deviant behavior among children, who lacked the parental supervision previously found in agrarian society. Of course, these schools had no models to draw on and it was a long time before they developed a uniform and viable structure. Collins describes the situation:

> Grade levels, the 4-year high school, the 8-year elementary school, and above all, regular yearly promotion, did not develop until the 1870s. There was considerable retardation in grade: As late as 1910, a majority of the students aged 14–17 were still in elementary school; approximately 25% of the elementary school population was over 13 years of age, 80% of secondary school students were over 18 . . . And colleges . . . had a range of students from their early teens to their mid-twenties. They did not require prior high school or even elementary school attendance as long as students were literate . . . and many colleges established their own preparatory departments for students who needed to work up these preparations.[20]

This unstructured arrangement appears disorganized by today's standards. Yet it can be taken as a model of a system that met the needs of individual people as opposed to the contemporary situation in which people are expected to adjust to the needs of the system. In any event, at the turn of the century, the educational administrator emerged as a new type of professional and the system underwent considerable change: grades were established and the curriculum was standardized; laws of compulsory attendance were passed and continually extended; and school districts were formed, which necessitated further bureaucratization. By the early 20th century, the contemporary primary and secondary school systems had assumed the shape by which they are recognized today. As Collins notes, it was "a unitary sequence, open and compulsory for all, preparing primarily for college education, rigidly age graded, with a heavy emphasis on moving students through in orderly phalanxes."[21]

When viewed in this light, it is possible to understand why contemporary primary and secondary schools are the way they are, especially in relation to the question of relevance, or the lack of direct connection with occupational preparation. From the perspective of bureaucratic efficiency, there is no sense preparing students for the working world until they are allowed onto the labor market. And this is defined partly by compulsory education and child labor laws, which often go hand in hand. The primary reason for keeping students in school for longer periods of time is not, therefore, to ensure that they are better trained, except for a minority that go on to highly specialized fields; it is for the sake of others, namely, schools and their employees, professional associations, and dominant economic interests. The latter particularly benefit from the indoctrination of entire generations as well as the sequestering of young people in schools. The sequestering protects the economic community from disruptions that might occur if young people were idle and it keeps them out of the labor force until they are needed.[22]

The university system grew out of similar entrepreneurial activity. In the United States, higher education more clearly emerged from the philosophy of free enterprise than state governance. Interestingly, the earliest colleges were primarily for religious training or for training in classics. They were not thought to be suitable places for transmitting occupational skills. Wealthy people patronized them for the most part and did so primarily for the status that a college education conferred. By the mid-1800s, there was a frenzy of entrepreneurial activity related to the establishment of private, profit-making colleges. However, of the 1,000 colleges founded in this period, 700 failed.[23] Thus, despite the fact that the secondary school system had been relatively standardized, college administrators could not entirely convince the public that they provided a worthwhile service.

By the 1880s, educational entrepreneurs finally realized that many people considered the classical education they offered irrelevant. More important, they reasoned that student life was not considered an enjoyable experience by many people because it required self-sacrifice and monastic dedication. So in the spirit of capitalism, the curriculum was changed to include sciences, social sciences, languages, literature, and so forth as part of an elective system.[24] To make campus life fun, the scholarly model gave way to the socializing model, which incorporated sports and varsity teams. The latter fostered school spirit and loyalty. Fraternities and sororities were openly encouraged to enhance this school spirit and to establish a link between the university and the career world (through the so-called old-boys' network). Hence, universities promised an exciting social life to those who enrolled.

These reforms were very attractive to the upper middle class, many of whom had earned their fortune in the new industrial economy. What better place to send their sons and daughters to find the "right" spouses, to meet others of similar backgrounds, and to help their children fight a malaise that might set in as they attempted to integrate into a disorganized society? It worked! Between 1850 and 1920 the number of colleges in the United States rose from 120 to 1,041. By 1970 the figure was 2,556. Meanwhile, educational administrators worked to further standardize grade progression, secondary school requirements, and subsequent advancement beyond the B.A. Collins provides this summary of what took place:

The universities thus consolidated their newly established prestige and firmly established the 4-year B.A. curriculum, or analogues of it in some vocational fields (engineering, business administration, education, nursing), as a universal stage in a sequence toward post-high-school certification. Whatever the amount of training necessary, 4 years of it was to be required; moreover, any field aspiring to high professional status must establish itself in the sequence after the B.A. . . . By the mid-twentieth century, the universities had realized a self-fulfilling prophecy. By continually harping on the unspecified but great usefulness of the college degree for "success," universities had succeeded in surviving, and growing until the point at which college education could be seen to have specific payoffs.[25]

Hence, we have the modern mass educational system in the United States. This system is not particularly "rational" in terms of either occupational training or personal development. But, it works to the advantage of those who make major decisions in Western societies. As Collins argues:

the lengthy courses of study required by business and professional schools exist in good part to raise the status of the profession and to form the barrier of socialization between practitioners and lay[persons]. The degree to which education provides mainly these status and socialization functions varies among occupations. It seems to be great in pharmacy, where the 4-year university course is felt by practitioners to be "good for the profession." . . .[26]

Unfortunately, the masses have not fully benefited from mass education.[27] The creation of this educational monopoly has had the effect of producing what we have called an education inflation (see chapter 2) by which the value of lower levels of education decreases as more individuals obtain higher levels. This makes it difficult for working-class and lower-middle-class youths to compete with those from more privileged backgrounds.

In response to education inflation, professional associations (for example, the American Medical Association) have required increasingly higher qualifications for entrance, thereby keeping enrollment in programs small and maintaining prestige and income levels. As a result, more people compete for educational credentials with less chance of success.

A moment of the inflationary cycle of credentialism is captured in chart 4.1, which reveals that about one-half of 1988 graduates from Canadian colleges and universities reenrolled in another educational program within two years. Chart 4.2 illustrates the range of underemployment that university graduates can expect. While those programs that most clearly equip students with job skills have the lowest levels of underemployment (e.g., engineering), these levels are still in the 20 to 30 percent range (as opposed to an overall level of 43 percent).

Clearly, we have arrived at the point where those who scramble for credentials must endure years of conditioning. But many of those who lose at the end of this scramble because of underemployment, also lose in a second way if they have been conditioned into a state of false consciousness. Either way, win or lose, this conditioning serves dominant economic interests because it trains students to become workers who accept various forms of unrewarding labor (hence the educational system's emphasis on discipline and unquestioning obedience).

When considered in this light, mass education in Western industrial societies can be interpreted as a mass indoctrination of students.[28] This indoctrination is part of a rigid training for the requirements of the industrial and business workplace, which often require punctuality, self-discipline, and an uncritical willingness to do whatever is required, no matter how demeaning, alienating, or unethical that may be. Such indoctrination also stifles signs of independent or critical thinking.

This disciplinary posture is intended to create fear among potential rebels and to condition them to accept blindly the

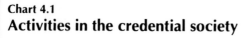

## Chart 4.1
## Activities in the credential society

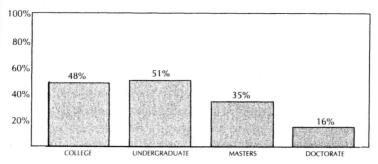

Note that about one-half of graduates from community colleges and under-graduate programs reenrolled in an educational program within two years of graduation.

From: Nobert, McDowell, and Goulet, 1992.

## Chart 4.2
## Underemployment among university graduates, by field of study, in Canada, 1988

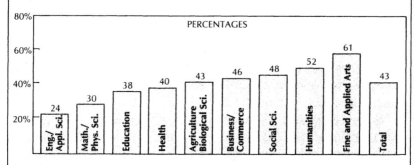

Note that of those who graduated in 1986, 43 percent reported in 1988 being in jobs that did not require university-level credentials. This under-employment varies by field of study but is still 24 percent in engineering and applied science, the most "successful" field.

From: Nobert, 1991.

legitimacy of the established authorities. Currently, the mass educational system has been granted about a decade and a half by the state to accomplish this task of social control. And, as noted above, it is continually being granted more time, ostensibly for the good of the student and the good of the society. As we have also argued, the attempt to manufacture consent also manufactures dissent. In the next chapter, we see that dissent among students has reached the point where guards are now needed to maintain order in some schools and lotteries are held to entice students to attend their classes.

Some of those who find themselves underemployed are also voicing their dissent, albeit in a constrained manner. The statistics cited regarding underemployment are brought to life in an article from our own university's student newspaper in which an underemployed university graduate expresses resentment toward the university system:

> Janet Lagace graduated from Western in 1991 with an honours degree in chemistry and a dream of becoming a lab technician. Two years later, Legace — working full-time as a manager of a variety store . . . — says it has been next to impossible to find a job in her field. "As soon as I got out of school, I applied all over, even out west," Lagace said. "I've worked damn hard, but every place wants three years (of) experience before they take you . . ."
>
> Lagace, who . . . received OSAP [Ontario Student Assistance Payments], said she is unable to afford going back to school because of her financial situation. "I received very generous OSAP loans, but I owed $15,000 (coming) out of school," she said. "Now I'm down to $10,000 and I will probably be paying it off for the next twenty years." Lagace blames her lack of success on the university education system, which she said offers a student no practical experience or training.
>
> "University does nothing for you once you're done. You have no skill. You learn to work hard and work independently, but it doesn't do you any good in the job market,"

she said. "I wasted five years of my life in university. At least with college you get some practical experience and don't get lost in space," she said. "But this is all hindsight. How do you know at the time? The entire guidance department (at my high school) kept telling me — go to university, go to university."[29]

Apparently, those like Janet Lagace escape the worst aspect of false consciousness where they blame themselves for their lack of success. Instead, they sense that they have been duped.

## THE MANUFACTURE OF DISSENT

When viewed from the perspective of the politics and ideology of language, notions such as freedom become problematic, and the freedoms that young people are said to enjoy appear illusory. In fact, the widespread resentment and alienation young people experience are signals that they are not immune from, or entirely unaware of, their mass disenfranchisement. Destructive street riots and violent gang warfare are only the most visible manifestations of their disaffection, which has been systematically produced as part of an attempt to manufacture a consensus among the young.

# 5

---

# Complementarity and the Social Control of Dissent

---

As we have noted, social control is generally believed to be highest in socialist societies where individual freedoms are virtually nonexistent, and where governments are forcibly imposed on citizens. This is the sense in which the public often equates totalitarian society with socialist society. Interestingly most readers presume that George Orwell's fictitious totalitarian society Oceania was really based on the former Soviet Union. After all, the absence of individual liberty and choice among the dystopia's inhabitants and the menacing intrusiveness of the government of Big Brother square very well with the images of life in the Soviet Union that were common in the West. However, Orwell may very well have been speaking of the West in his condemnation of Oceania as a totalitarian society:

> With the absorption of Europe by Russia and the British Empire by the United States, two of the three existing powers, Eurasia and Oceania, were already effectively in being . . . . Oceania comprises the Americas, the Atlantic islands

including the British Isles, Australasia, and the southern portion of Africa.[1]

The possibility that all those subtle and not-so-subtle forms of manipulation and control in Oceania actually apply to the West has to be somewhat disconcerting to those who always equated totalitarianism and dictatorship with Communist society. But, as we have argued, herein lies one of the principal benefits of ideological control: the controlled are not even aware of the fact that they are controlled, and as a consequence, they offer little or no resistance to it. In other words, it is important from the perspective of maintaining social order and the status quo for the disenfranchised segments of Western society to entertain the fiction that they are free while others are not.

With this in view, Aldous Huxley could very well have been talking about young people in contemporary Western culture when he observes in *Brave New World* that "A really efficient totalitarian state would be one in which the all-powerful executive of political bosses and their army of managers control a population of slaves who do not have to be coerced, because they love their servitude."[2]

The apathy, alienation, and disaffection of today's youth make them unwitting pawns in a system that does not really respect them. From the viewpoint of those in control, however, the secret is to not have the young recognize their servitude as servitude, or their apathy as apathy. This touches on the earlier discussion of the politics of language. For if servitude to the system could be defined as freedom to choose and to spend their money on an endless array of youth-identity items such as $200 running shoes, compact discs, and designer clothes, then the need to resort to physical coercion disappears. Furthermore, if apathy is defined as freedom *not* to participate meaningfully in the dominant social institutions, as in the case of the moratorium period discussed in chapter 3, then the task of social control is complete. The controlled (youth) remain oblivious of their manipulation and disenfranchisement.

But how is this acceptance of the status quo engineered? Huxley explains: "To make them love it is the task assigned, in present-day totalitarian states, to ministries of propaganda, newspaper editors and schoolteachers."[3] We contend that this form of social engineering is akin to the situation in Western, liberal democratic countries today. For those who live in the West are not without newspaper and TV editors who censor and sanitize the news; schoolteachers who indoctrinate students; and "ministries of propaganda" that package politicians and sell everything from pet rocks to vacation trips to the moon.

The point Huxley makes, then, is valid for totalitarian societies and also for various Western societies where control and manipulation of the populations are more subtle, more cleverly disguised. That this is not usually seen to apply to the latter societies, however, testifies to the fact that it is ideologically masked in those societies. Huxley outlines the insidious way in which the Cold War was orchestrated following the Second World War:

> By simply not mentioning certain subjects, by lowering what Mr. Churchill calls an "iron curtain" between the masses and such facts or arguments as the political bosses regard as undesirable, totalitarian propogandists have influenced opinion much more effectively than they could have done by the most eloquent denunciations, the most compelling of logical rebuttals.[4]

In the case of youth in contemporary capitalist society, the propagandists and opinion-makers — politicians, news media, teachers, advertisers, and the massive entertainment industry — resemble the powers that be in the socialist societies. The plan is clear: disenfranchised and potentially disruptive groups must be kept oblivious of their true situation. And the most efficient way to distract them is through ideology — whether one is dealing with ideologies of nationalism, racism, sexism, or any other such body of beliefs and ideas that appeals to people's emotions and stirs them up. In other words, a distracted population benefits or complements the interests of those who wish to rule. But what exactly does *complementary* mean in this context?

## THE PRINCIPLE OF COMPLEMENTARITY

From the perspective of those who occupy positions of authority, it is important to use force only as a last resort. This stands to reason, since force engenders resentment and could potentially lead to a rule that is continually contested, whether in an overt or a clandestine manner. The challenge for the successful rulers, then, is to secure the consent of the ruled, especially in situations where the latter do not stand to benefit. In Huxley's terms, it involves the political question of getting the slaves to love their servitude; or, in Marxian terms creating a state of false consciousness in which the slaves do not even realize that they are slaves.

To fully understand the manner in which this is effected, we need to examine the concept of complementarity as it is elaborated in the writings of Bernd Baldus,[5] where it is closely related to concerns with social control and legitimacy. Baldus argues that social control can be effected in one of two ways: either physically via the deliberate intervention of some body or agency or more subtly and ideologically by the manipulation of what he calls "complementary conditions." Physical and ideological control differ in both form and content. Ideological control is slower to effect, more indirect, less easily resisted, but more difficult to escape once it is established. Similarly, those who are subject to ideological control tend to be less aware of the fact than those who are physically controlled. This makes the former more effective.

As a strategy of control, the manipulation of complementary conditions involves either the use of existing patterns of behavior within the population and society at large or the deliberate creation of such behavior patterns. More concretely, those in control observe the behavior of specific target populations, noting whether it complements or furthers their interests. Where it is complementary it will be encouraged, used, or exploited; and where certain patterns of behavior do not exist, those in power will attempt to ascertain the possibilities of creating them. This is the model of social control portrayed by Huxley. On the other hand, where a behavior exists that appears inimical to the dominant interests, steps will be taken to modify or eliminate it; but this is often more related to the question of physical force. This is the model of social control portrayed by Orwell.[6]

Baldus sees an example of the deliberate use of complementarity in Philip Agee's *Inside the Company*.[7] As an ex-CIA agent, Agee was in a position to give incisive insights to the daily operations of the American Central Intelligence Agency. The CIA, we are told, was very calculating in its search for preexisting complementary conditions such as conservative, anti-civil rights sentiments among the public. And having discovered them, the agency was forthcoming with financial support for conservative parties. It also fed false information to local mass media concerning the aims of leftist political movements, and covered up the real identities of those who were behind the bombings of black churches. This sort of activity, Baldus contends, was conducted "in such a way that it is likely to be attributed to 'radical subversives,' [and] takes advantage of existing conditions which are favourable to the Agency's goals."[8]

Thus, the CIA played upon the fundamental conservatism of the American people and used their fear and suspicion of radical politics to discredit the civil rights movement and other political causes that criticized the establishment. But while the climate of fear and suspicion was not directly created by the CIA, its prior existence represented "important complements essential to the success of the Agency's operations" by contributing to the delegitimization of such movements.

We may also refer to Orwell's *Nineteen Eighty-Four* for another example of the use of complementarity. Among the so-called proles (the working class) of Oceania, who made up 85 percent of the total population of three hundred million, Orwell tells us that there existed a fairly high level of apathy. Even the mass rallies were very carefully orchestrated and had a clear superficiality to them. The proles were fatalistic, apolitical, and resigned to their lot in life. They were interested only in the petty and irrelevant details of daily life. In fact, as Winston, the protagonist, remarks after an aborted conversation with a prole: "The old man's memory was nothing but a rubbish-heap of details. One could question him all day without getting any real information."[9]

How different are people today from the proles of Oceania? Young people's indifference to social and political issues certainly complements the interests of the dominant class, for they seldom challenge the rule of the latter.[10] During the 1980s, there was much talk of the "me generation," which points to an ascendance of the ideology of individualism and a preoccupation with financial well-being. Unlike the 1960s when youths sought to find meaning in relationships with others and to explore alternative philosophies, we have witnessed over the past 20 years a disengagement from these existential issues.

Chart 5.1 presents results from the "largest and longest continuing study of American higher education. Each year some 550 institutions and roughly 270,000 students participate in the survey."[11] Note that between 1967 and 1986 the predominant values of "developing a meaningful philosophy of life" and "being very well-off financially" have almost traded places. Between 1970 and 1984, out of a list of 17 other personal values, "being financially very well-off [rose] from ninth to second place. . . ."[12] This study suggests just how effective the consent-manufacturing mechanisms have been in transforming young people's values so that they are more complementary to dominant interests.

Generally speaking, then, young people are encouraged to narrow their thinking and to focus on issues of personal materialism and consumerism, from which big business is the principal beneficiary. As a consequence, their pursuits have become self-centered and linked to immediate gratification. Studies in the United States show that between 1953 and 1983 part-time employment among male high-school students has increased from about 29 percent to 36 percent and from 18 percent to 36 percent for females.[13] While some

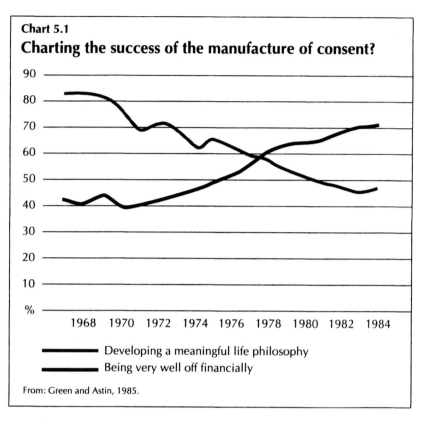

**Chart 5.1**

**Charting the success of the manufacture of consent?**

Developing a meaningful life philosophy

Being very well off financially

From: Green and Astin, 1985.

might interpret this trend as an indication of increasing independence, it appears that most students fritter away their earnings. As Fine, Mortimer, and Roberts note, "when asked about their motivations for employment, [high-school students] emphasize the monetary rewards," and most of their discretionary income "supports a high level of self-indulgent consumption." Ninth-graders spend their money primarily on clothing (among 70 percent of those studied), and secondarily on items like "records, tapes, sports equipment, stereos, TVs, bikes," and various forms of entertainment. Only "22% were saving for their future education, and only 7% admitted giving money to their families."[14]

Not only does mindless consumption divert attention from larger concerns, it has become a driving force of the advanced capitalist economy. As we saw in the last chapter, entrepreneurs know exactly how much discretionary income the youth market has and they target it by "appropriating the indigenous symbols of youth leisure, rebellion, and revolt, and translate them into consumer goods" like black leather jackets and blue jeans. Moreover, according to Fine, Mortimer, and Roberts, the music industry "has been largely underwritten by teenagers' cash" and one of its appeals is that, like sports, music holds the promise of a meteoric rise to fame, which young people can fantasize about.[15] Hence, the music industry plays a similar role to lotteries in Orwell's Oceania by providing escape fantasies.

Among young people a major emphasis is increasingly placed on the creation of a "feel-good" existence, with little regard for long-term objectives. Young people can now escape into technological "trivial pursuits" that entertain them while leaving the power structure intact. But this is no accident and the young are not to blame. As we have said, indifference complements the dominant economic and political interests, and this is why it has been systematically manufactured by the principal social institutions: the educational system, the mass media, and the entertainment industry. The way in which youth experience is structured today recalls *Brave New World*, a world in which all organizations and activities are designed to either produce or consume something.

As noted in chapter 1, Tinning and Fitzclarence argue that many of the processes we have discussed are spreading to other countries because of technological advances that are creating a global postmodern market. They submit that while older institutions such as the family, education, and the workplace still play significant roles in the lives of the young "in postmodernity, the media play a primary role as a mediator for each of these social organizations." They add that young people's "very perceptions of, and experiences within, each are shaped to a greater or lesser extent by experiences with information technology such as television, telephone, FM radio, video, and computer." In a society where the young seek that immediate gratification and are intellectually passive, teachers find it difficult to motivate them. Moreover, this influence is rapidly spreading around the global village: "Postmodern adolescent life in Geelong, Australia, is increasingly linked to life in Los Angeles, Tokyo, and Berlin."[16]

Similarly, Hargreaves and Goodson argue that because of these postmodern technologies,

> many of today's youth live in a world where reality tries to live up to its images, [reality] becomes suffused with images, [and] may be indistinguishable from its images. Technologically, textbooks, worksheets and overheads are a poor match for these other more complex, instantaneous and sometimes spectacular forms of experience and learning. . . . At the same time, there is a danger that the spectacle and superficiality of an instantaneous visual culture may supersede and obliterate the necessary moral discourse and studied reflection of a more oral one.[17]

To return to our Orwellian analogy, the lesson to be learned is that it is critical for those in power to distract the masses so that they remain oblivious of their fettered state and do not rise up in protest. Orwell spoke of how the government of Big Brother was able to use the pervasive mood of apathy among the proles, who were "without general ideas," to realize its program of mass control. By staging public events such as the Lottery, which served even more to distract the proles from the reality of their condition, Big Brother was able to maintain the status quo. The Lottery, with its weekly payout of enormous prizes, was one event to which the workers paid serious attention. It gave them a raison d'être:

> It was their delight, their folly, their anodyne, their intellectual stimulant. Where the Lottery was concerned, even people who could barely read or write were capable of intricate calculations and staggering feats of memory. There was a whole tribe of men who made a living simply by selling systems, forecasts and lucky amulets.[18]

Again, this state of affairs anticipates what has happened in many Western countries. For example, illiteracy in Canada has reached epidemic proportions — as many as 40 percent of those who begin high school either drop out or graduate as functional illiterates (i.e., they cannot perform the basic reading and arithmetic tasks required for independent functioning). According to Hargreaves and Goodson, "15% of Canadians [aged] 16–19 . . . [can]not read well enough to deal with most of the written material encountered in everyday life. A further 23% [can] carry out simple reading tasks but [can]not read more complex material."[19] They report similar statistics for numeracy.[20] Moreover, in spite of massive public expenditures, our educational system has degenerated to the point where students are literally being bribed to attend classes. A recent newspaper article discusses a pilot project at Bonnie Doon High School in Edmonton, which remunerated teenagers for coming to class:

> In a program that school officials believe is a first in Canada, the students at Bonnie Doon are being rewarded with cash and prizes for simply showing up for school regularly and on time. It is called the Miss School-Miss Out Program and it is a derivative of a similar program that was developed in Spokane, Wash., as a way of cutting down on high-school truancy.
>
> The concept is simple. The school year is divided into four quarters, and at the end of each the students who have perfect attendance are entered into a lottery for prizes that have been donated by businesses. The winnings so far have included hot-air balloon rides, scholarships, $100 in loonies, dinner at McDonald's and, best of all, a free day off school for everyone who makes the grade. The idea is to attach a material reward for good attendance, something that has traditionally been encouraged through the threat of detentions, suspensions and, in the old days, the strap.
>
> Yet facing an empty classroom seat has been one of the most frustrating problems facing the nation's high-school teachers. At Bonnie Doon, Mr. Bjarnason says that 10 to 15 per cent of the school population can be absent on any given day. It is worse in other places, he says. The dilemma

this presents to teachers is obvious: If a student isn't there to listen, no amount of good, innovative teaching is going to make a difference and help reverse the decision of one in four of Canada's high schoolers to drop out.

In the first year of the program, offering material payoffs for good attendance seems to be working at Bonnie Doon. The school's honour roll has more than doubled. About a quarter of the school's 650 students managed to achieve attendance records that qualified them for the prizes — which are usually abundant enough so everyone gets one — and 95 percent of those saw their grades improve.[21]

We also know that while great numbers of young males contribute to a multimillion dollar industry that produces hockey, football, baseball, and basketball cards, and while they can recite the batting, catching, pitching, and scoring statistics of individual players, many of them cannot even recite their multiplication tables. The same applies to those who know every lyric of the top 10 songs in any given week and yet cannot recite a poem.

In a sense, then, the proles of Oceania appear not to be very different from their counterparts in today's North America, where the lottery mentality is firmly entrenched among those who hope to strike it rich overnight.[22] But lotteries are not the only events that distract youth and other powerless segments of Western society. The entertainment and sports industries also serve this end. For in addition to the video revolution in music and arcade games, and Walkmans which enable the individual to tune out the world, the public is bombarded with flashy concert tours, the pomp and ceremony of which are matched only by the highest levels of sporting events: the Superbowl, the Grey Cup, the Stanley Cup, the World Series, the National Basketball Association (NBA) finals, and National Collegiate Amateur Athletic (NCAA) confrontations.

With salaries that surpass those of the highest-paid politicians and businesspersons, movie stars and athletes become the idols of the young. They belong to a glamorous world that the average individual dreams about joining. These dreams are fueled by the "rags to riches" stories that explain the stars' ascent to fame and lead the young to believe that their fantasies can be realized.

This mythology is especially prevalent regarding black athletes. However, according to Donald Sabo and Sue Jansen, in the United States "only about 3,000 blacks make their living at professional sports, [including] coaches and management personnel. Indeed, there is greater probability for a black high school athlete to become a doctor than a professional athlete." Sabo and Jansen go on to argue that modern sports are the "real-life analogue . . . [of] capitalist ideology," where there is the belief that "all players begin the game at the same starting point, but the most talented finish first." The reality of capitalism, however, is that not everyone has "the same starting point, teams are not evenly matched, and the scoring system does not necessarily reward skill, training, intelligence, or determination."[23] Thus, professional sports serve to perpetuate the myth that life is fair, an illusion necessary to the status quo.

When the masses remain distracted and uninformed, the job of controlling them is that much easier. And because distraction and ignorance complement the interests of those in control, it is easy to see why the entertainment and sporting industries are so important: they make billions of dollars for those who run them and, from a political point of view, they are useful as distractions. This is not to say, however, that such things as sports and movies were designed specifically for this purpose; rather, they are examples of behaviors and practices that exist already and which are complementary to the interests of those in control. But conversely, if such conditions did not exist beforehand, they could be created via the manipulation of such institutions as public education systems and the mass media, as is the case with lotteries.

The use of complementarity as a strategy of social control, then, benefits the dominant interests in two ways. First, it manages to induce needed behavior at costs that are much lower than those that would be incurred if the same behavior were to be created through force — by using police, courts, prisons, or the military. Clearly, a dilemma is faced by social control agents when conventional methods break down and force emerges as the only alternative. In Canada, the prospect of using force to keep order in secondary schools is still viewed as unpalatable and somewhat un-Canadian, although in many American schools it is now commonplace. However, such control would undoubtedly be welcomed by the 40 percent of Canadian high-school students who agree that "the two problems of gangs and school violence have now reached a 'very serious' stage."[24]

Similarly, a recent opinion poll revealed that 53 percent of Canadians now want security guards in schools. In writing about this issue Lynne Ainsworth noted that the police are hesitant to take up such a role. In Toronto, though, police were called on to deal with 1,000 incidents in schools during 1990, a 16 percent rise from 1989. Because many of these incidents involved weapons, the situation is now one of "grave concern" to Toronto police, so they may have little choice. Ainsworth also quotes Staff Sergeant Steven Duggan's remark that the "'next 10 years are going to be critical ones for our youth.'" Duggan also sees that a major problem in dealing with school violence is that most victims will not come forward: "'Only 1 in 20 youths (affected by violence) are coming forward and telling their story because the kids have no faith in the adult system. They'd rather try and solve the problem themselves.'"[25]

The second benefit of the complementarity approach relates to the fact that the dominant interests are served while simultaneously permitting a wide range of behaviors among the population at large to continue. For as Baldus observes, "complementary behavior is judged primarily by its instrumentality or utility for dominant class interests."[26] Hence, it does not matter if the proles in Orwell's Oceania or the youth of today attribute meanings to their behavior that are totally different from those assigned by the dominant interests. The only thing that matters is that their behavior does not run counter to those interests. Speaking of the proles, Orwell says that the mundane details of their daily lives were of no importance to Big Brother, provided that they did not conflict with the aims of the authorities. Thus, they were generally left to themselves, free to revert to a style of life that was natural to them:

> They were born, they grew up in the gutters, they went to work at twelve, they passed through a brief blossoming period of beauty and sexual desire, they married at twenty, they were middle-aged at thirty, they died, for the most part, at sixty. Heavy physical work, the care of home and children, petty quarrels with neighbours, films, football, beer, and above all, gambling filled up the horizon of their minds. To keep them in control was not difficult.[27]

Again, by extrapolation, what is important in the case of today's youth is not the subjective meanings attached to their behavior; rather, it is the outcome. For example, if they think that their rap music, which criticizes the system, provides an outlet for their discontent and brings them satisfaction, that is fine. As long as their protests go nowhere, they are left alone; recording companies produce and sell their records, and everyone is happy.

However, if the young rappers choose to act on the message of their lyrics, then it is a different matter and force is used. Imbued with a sense of their liberal freedoms, which include the freedom of speech, these young people claim the right to sing about any themes and to be as outrageous and violent as they wish in their lyrics. Their right to do so is even defended by the establishment's invoking of the freedom-of-speech guarantees that form the basis of all liberal democratic constitutions, and this is why occasional calls for censorship are seldom heeded. The point, however, is that the illusion of freedom contained in the right of free speech distracts the youths in question from realizing that theirs is often an empty freedom. They may decry the injustices of the system in their songs as long as they do not endanger the right of others to pursue life, liberty, and happiness. In other words, the notion of freedom embodied in such "rights" as free speech, free association, and freedom of the press merely placates the powerless by leading them to believe that they are free and equal with others in the society when, in fact, they are not. Freedom thus conceived is ideological.

## COMPLEMENTARITY AND NATIONALISM: AN EXAMPLE

An illustration of how ideology can distract people from appreciating what may be in their own best interests, and allow the rule of the oppressor to go unchallenged, can be seen in the context of nationalism, particularly during times of war. As an ideology, nationalism transcends racial, sexual, political, and class boundaries and serves to unite an otherwise divided population in defense of a common ideal.[28] Witness, for example, the reactions of Argentine and British citizens to the 1982 conflict over the Malvinas, or Falkland Islands. Putting aside the very grave domestic economic and political problems in their respective countries, both these populations rallied passionately around their respective governments and went to war for an idea, one that evoked a sense of patriotism and pride in their homelands.

In Argentina the military dictatorship temporarily did not have to worry about the soaring unemployment rate, which was over 40 percent, or inflation that topped the 200 percent mark, or daily protests against its practice of murdering political opponents. All segments of society, including political prisoners, who were freed for the occasion, were mobilized in support of the goal of national integrity and dignity. The Argentines were determined to repel the British, because their continued possession of the Malvinas symbolized an affront to Argentine national pride.[29]

In Britain, where Margaret Thatcher's political fortunes and popularity had been sinking to unprecedented depths, the people's response was similar. Tens of thousands of young men rushed to enlist and travel halfway around the world to defend their country's honor. The prime minister's decision to go to war in defense of Britain's isolated colonial possession in the South Atlantic Ocean met with wide approval domestically, and after winning the battle over the Falklands, Britons were able to bask in the glow of patriotism and were prepared to overlook the economic conditions that, before the war, had threatened to bring down the Conservative government. Consequently, not too long after the war, Thatcher was able to call an election and obtain a landslide victory. The British Labour Party (the Opposition) was stunned.

The plot for the Argentine–British confrontation could have been derived from Orwell's portrayal of political life in Oceania. In that society's ongoing war against Eastasia and Eurasia alternately, the citizens were constantly on guard against the threat of foreign invasion. The fear of invasion distracted them from more immediate domestic problems so that the authorities did not have to worry about local uprisings against their rule:

> All that was required of them (the proles) was a primitive patriotism which could be appealed to whenever it was necessary to make them accept longer working hours or short rations. And even when they became discontented, their discontent led nowhere, because being without general ideas, they could only focus it on petty specific grievances. The larger evils invariably escaped their notice.[30]

Through the phrase "primitive patriotism," Orwell hints at a blind, even primordial, devotion to the idea of a homeland that nurtures and sustains all of its citizens. Indeed, so emotionally charged is the presumed allegiance that anyone who questions it is deemed unpatriotic and treacherous. But how fictional or farfetched is Orwell's vision?

## THE COMPLEMENTARITY OF NATIONALISM AND RACE IN THE UNITED STATES

The United States supplies an ideal context in which to explore the following question: Given the deep-seated racial divisions in that country, do young African Americans see themselves as African first and American second? Or are they American first and African second? It is most instructive to examine the observation we made earlier about the power of nationalism to transcend internal social divisions by asking these questions in the context of the recent Persian Gulf War. That war was declared and stopped by the president of the United States, who only paid lip service to the United Nations.[31] The three official reasons given for the involvement were: to make the world safe for democracy;[32] to protect vital American commercial and financial interests (namely, the supply of oil that is so crucial to American industry); and to safeguard American jobs that would be lost if unpredictable Iraq were allowed to swallow up Kuwait's vast oil fields.

At the height of the hostilities the United States had committed some 600,000 troops, which exceeded the combined representation of all its allies by almost a half million. As we know, however, the patriotic zeal with which the American offensive was embraced managed to override the voices of most detractors, who were keen to point out that while blacks make up about 14 to 15 percent of the nation's population, young black servicemen and women made up well over 30 percent of the forces in the Persian Gulf. Add to this the fact that not a single American senator or congressional representative, who are overwhelmingly white (and male), had a child in the Persian Gulf, and an interesting picture emerges.

As we know, poverty in the United States is tragically high within the black community. So, too, are its associated ills: unemployment, crime, illiteracy, malnutrition, and so forth. Indeed, as previously noted, in the United States there are more college-aged black males in prison than in college. This is made even more disturbing when one realizes that it would be far cheaper to send these young men to college than to keep them in prison.

But how was the involvement of blacks in the Persian Gulf War orchestrated?

To begin, those black spokespersons who opposed the war were dubbed "un-American," for pointing out the fact that a) a disproportionate number of black soldiers were risking their lives to "liberate" Kuwaitis in Kuwait, when they themselves were prisoners of racism and poverty in the United

States, and b) the billions of dollars being spent on the war could easily have been put toward eradicating poverty in the United States.[33] In addition, however, we were presented with a very high-ranking black general, Colin Powell, who appeared constantly at the side of the president, and who, for the duration of the war, the major news networks were touting as a presidential candidate for the next election. This was meant to play upon the sentiment of national unity and also to give blacks the idea that the war was being fought for all Americans, not just by black Americans for white America. The upshot was that the war was fought and won in glamorous Hollywood style, and black and white voters together gave the president and his administration a rating in the 80 percent range. For all intents and purposes, appeals to patriotic and nationalist solidarity proved decisive over separatist and racial considerations.

In the context of the Gulf War a parallel can be drawn between the citizens of the United States and the proles. For in the same way that the people of Oceania were never sure who their enemy was — today Eastasia, tomorrow Eurasia — the citizens of the United States must also have been confused. Iraq was their ally against Iran in the first part of the 1980s, but by the end of the decade, as we have mentioned, the situation was reversed: Iraq became the enemy and secret deals were being worked out by senior American government officials with Iran. As yet the contradiction has not been explained to the American people. But worse, there does not appear to be a loud chorus of voices demanding one. We are back again to the apathy of which Orwell spoke and the fact that an apathetic population is most complementary to the interests of those in authority.

## YOUTH, COMPLEMENTARITY, AND THE MASS MEDIA

Young people are enthusiastic consumers of many products of the mass media. Concerns over the messages the media direct at them date back to the introduction of novels, comic books, movies, popular music, magazines, and, more recently, video games. Most of this apprehension involves the fear that some sort of moral degeneration will take place when young people are exposed to so-called adult themes. We do not advocate shielding young people from adult material; rather, our concern lies with how this material indoctrinates the young into an ethos based on consumerism, conformity, and immediate gratification. As we have argued, dominant interests have shaped these media to produce such an ethos, and in the process have prevented the young from developing a critical consciousness that would allow them to contemplate larger issues of personal and social responsibility.

In chapter 4 we discussed teenzines and noted that these encourage young women to intensify their feminine characteristics with cosmetics and fashionable clothing. One way of responding to the prevalence of these magazines is to argue that they are simply meeting a market need because young women want them. Another way would be to say that these magazines are specifically engineered to create a consciousness among young women, which is then defined as a need. As evidence of the latter position, we can examine the relationship between advertisers and publishers.

Most magazines depend upon advertising for their survival. In fashion magazines, it appears that advertisers often call the shots, so to speak. Susan Basow argues that in the case of adult women's magazines, advertisers "require a certain [amount] of 'complementary copy' for each of their ads, such as an article about hairstyling to accompany advertising for hair products." This explains why up to 90 percent of such magazines as *Glamour* and *Family Circle* contain ads and ad-related copy. It is also common for advertisers to refuse to advertise if they feel articles are unsympathetic to their products. Basow cites several examples of this: "Clairol withdrew its advertising from *Ms.* magazine after *Ms.* reported on a congressional hearing into the carcinogenic potential of hair dyes, and Estée Lauder refused to advertise there because no articles on makeup appeared in the magazine."[34] Thus, the content of women's magazines is largely dictated by the interests of advertisers. If these magazines are to survive, they have little choice but to comply. One notable exception to this is *Ms.*, which no longer finances itself with ads.

The control advertisers wield over the various media varies by degree, but few people would dispute that advertisers have an interest in producing an ethos of consumption.[35] One example of the extent to which the consumer ethos has penetrated the youth media comes from a Canadian television program called *Street Cents.* Chart 5.2 provides a copy of an advertisement flyer for the program that was circulated in Canadian banks shortly before it first aired. At first glance, the program appears benign, designed to help young teenagers manage their money. Note, however, the small TV set in the logo with the balloon caption that says "Buy it!" We believe that this caption reveals the real purpose of the television program, namely, to promote a consumer consciousness among young people that is not in their best interest. If there were a genuine concern for their welfare, many other topics would be dealt with, including career and educational planning, social responsibility, interpersonal relationships, and self-development. Instead of using the airwaves to condition young people to spend money they do not have, the media could focus on helping them to develop their intellect and a sense of social responsibility. Since they are bombarded with tantalizing images of the "good life," it is not surprising that the young are dispirited by the reality of their poor economic prospects.[36]

Thus far we have seen that the mass media share a vested interest in creating and maintaining a certain consciousness among the young. Some of these media do so as a concession to other economic interests, such as advertisers, while others do it directly for themselves (e.g., the music industry, including MuchMusic and MTV, channels devoted entirely to selling popular music). What lies at the heart of all this activity, however, is the fact that these media can sell young people some element of an identity that they have been taught to crave. This can happen because the possibility for a more meaningful identity has been denied young people through a series of laws, customs, and institutional practices. Conse-

**Chart 5.2**
**Indoctrination into consumerism?**

CBC Television and The Canadian Bankers' Association proudly present **Street Cents**, a new consumer affairs series for young people beginning on Saturday, October 7.

**Street Cents** is a fun and fast-paced program of consumer information and entertainment, designed to instil good buying sense, prudent judgement and consumer awareness in Canadian teens and pre-teens. Three young people will host the program, showing viewers how to save and make the most of their money. The program will regularly feature food reports, product surveys, and views from the marketing and advertising worlds.

The Canadian Bankers' Association is the major sponsor of **Street Cents**. Other contributors include The Royal Canadian Mint, Air Canada, and the consumer affairs or education ministries of the provinces.

The 30-minute programs started on Saturday, October 7. Air times are 10:00 a.m. in Central and Western Canada, 11:00 a.m. in the Maritimes, and 11:30 a.m. in Newfoundland.

quently, leisure industries such as music, fashion, and cosmetics now have a largely uncritical army of consumers awaiting the next craze or fad. Each fad gives them a sense of identity, however illusory or fleeting. This activity is tolerated or encouraged by larger economic interests because the army of willing consumers also serves as a massive reserve of cheap labor. Furthermore, distracting young people with these "trivial identity pursuits" prevents them from protesting against their impoverished condition.

Thus, the media play a key role in effecting social control by stifling dissent among a potentially powerful and disruptive segment of the population. They provide outlets for harmless forms of dissent, such as outrageous clothing, hairstyles, and music. However, young people are beginning to express their anger in more threatening ways, for example, by forming armed gangs that wage wars on the streets of today's inner cities. If this continues, the dissent that has been manufactured may come back to haunt the manufacturers.

Complementary behavior, in summary, contributes to the preservation of social order by giving those without power, such as the young, the impression that they are indeed empowered and can pursue goals of their own choosing, free from outside interference. It is important to cultivate this illusion, for it leaves the power structure intact and says to the young people that they are personally responsible for their situations in life. If the overall system is portrayed as free, open, and fair, and individuals believe they are masters of their own destinies, then there are no reasonable grounds on which youth and other disenfranchised groups can find fault with the system and its guardians. The legitimacy of the latter is secured on the basis of the very logic that says that order and control benefit everyone in the society. The less conscious one is of being controlled, and the more one feels in charge of one's destiny, the more effective is that control and the more secure that order. The very close relationship, then, among ideology, social control, and social order is evident.

# 6

## Toward a New Reality for Youth

As we have seen, the roots of youth disenfranchisement appear to lie in transformations in the industrial-capitalist economy, particularly the growth of the subordinate service sector and the concomitant decline of the agricultural sector.[1] But the change in industrial capitalism alone did not cause the disenfranchisement. Other factors have contributed to this problem: dominant economic interests have exploited the labor of young people to increase their profits and have viewed them as a large market on which to unload their products, showing no regard for their personal well-being; the "custodial professions" (teachers, psychologists, psychiatrists, and social workers employed by schools, prisons, and mental hospitals) have turned youth into their "clients" to be serviced for an ever-increasing period of time; people who have seniority by virtue of their age have sought higher wages and more power at the expense of the young; and governments have accommodated the interests of these sectors when drafting policies and implementing reforms.

Because we have been dealing with liberal democracies, where politicians — and their policies — can ostensibly be voted in and out of office, we will now focus on government-led initiatives regarding youth policies. We do this to draw

151

attention to a policy model that is more welcoming to young people than is the case in Canada and the United States. It is in the public policy arena that a "reenfranchising" of the young can be most immediately stimulated; and if the state supports the reenfranchisement of youth, other sectors of society will be more likely to follow.

## SWEDEN AS A MODEL

In capitalist societies, large-scale economic transformations, such as the rise of the service sector, are often zero-sum in nature. That is, the gains of certain parties are equal to the losses of other parties so that the net outcome is zero. Unfortunately, as we saw in chapter 2, young people have been the losers in the wake of recent economic transformations in countries such as the United States and Canada. In this concluding chapter, we show that the losses of the young have not been as great in other Western countries undergoing this transformation. Accordingly, we can take lessons from those countries, especially Sweden.

Sweden is one of the most prosperous, advanced industrial societies in the world. Certainly, it has been affected by the transformations that have taken place in other nations' economies — the processes that disenfranchise the young also exist there — but the Swedish government has grappled with this problem in a way that one would expect of enlightened political leaders. While Sweden, too, has a myriad of competing economic interest groups, it has been able to produce effective social policies aimed at the young. Thus, Sweden provides other liberal democracies with a model of what they can do to address the problems outlined in this book.

The country's long history of experimentation with social policies prepared it well for the difficulties facing its young. These policies have been designed to ensure that Sweden is a compassionate society with a high standard of living. Countries like the United States maintain a high standard overall, but large disparities exist within the population. In other words, social policy in America tends to be based on a "win-lose" model, while in Sweden it is based more on a "win-win" one.

The most direct evidence of the youth-disenfranchisement process in Sweden can be found in unemployment and wage statistics. Over the past several decades, the unemployment rate for those aged 16 to 24 has hovered at about twice the rate of the labor force as a whole. Table 6.1 presents the figures for 1971 to 1981. But note how *low* these rates are for *all* age groups in comparison with North American rates (see charts 2.9 and 2.10). Sweden's long-standing policy of full employment, which dates back to the 1930s, is responsible for these very low rates.

Given the Swedes' commitment to full employment, even small increases in their low unemployment rate concern them greatly. So the government took action immediately during the worldwide recession of the early 1980s to wrestle the rate back down to an acceptable level. Table 6.2 focuses on youth unemployment and shows how the rate fluctuated for the period 1978 to 1988. While the recession of the early 1990s has produced a small rise in this rate,[2] there is clear evidence that Sweden managed to reverse this aspect of the disenfranchisement process.

**Table 6.1**

**Unemployment rates in Sweden by age category, 1971–1981**

|      | 16–24 | 25–54 | 55–66 |
| ---- | ----- | ----- | ----- |
| 1971 | 5.1   | 1.8   | 2.8   |
| 1972 | 5.7   | 2.0   | 2.5   |
| 1973 | 5.3   | 1.8   | 2.4   |
| 1974 | 4.4   | 1.3   | 2.3   |
| 1975 | 3.8   | 1.0   | 1.9   |
| 1976 | 3.7   | 1.1   | 1.6   |
| 1977 | 4.4   | 1.3   | 1.3   |
| 1978 | 5.5   | 1.4   | 1.8   |
| 1979 | 5.0   | 1.4   | 1.9   |
| 1980 | 5.1   | 1.4   | 1.6   |
| 1981 | 5.4   | 1.8   | 2.0   |

Source: *Statistical Abstracts of Sweden*, National Bureau of Statistics, 1981.

**Table 6.2**

**Unemployment rates for young people in Sweden, 1978–1988**

|       | 16   | 17   | 18   | 19   | 20–24 | 25+ |
|-------|------|------|------|------|-------|-----|
| 1978  | 9.5  | 9.9  | 7.4  | 6.4  | 4.3   | 1.6 |
| 1979  | 9.9  | 9.1  | 7.2  | 5.3  | 3.7   | 1.5 |
| 1980  | 9.8  | 9.0  | 7.6  | 5.5  | 3.7   | 1.4 |
| 1981  | 11.5 | 10.1 | 10.0 | 7.6  | 4.7   | 1.8 |
| 1982  | 9.0  | 11.1 | 11.9 | 9.6  | 6.1   | 2.4 |
| 1983  | 7.2  | 8.3  | 13.1 | 10.2 | 6.8   | 2.7 |
| 1984  | 4.8  | 6.5  | 5.2  | 3.9  | 6.6   | 2.6 |
| 1985  | 4.0  | 5.6  | 5.5  | 3.5  | 6.3   | 2.3 |
| 1986  | 2.6  | 5.0  | 4.6  | 3.8  | 6.2   | 2.1 |
| 1987  | 3.7  | 3.5  | 3.8  | 3.3  | 4.4   | 1.5 |
| 1988  | 4.3  | 3.2  | 2.9  | 2.7  | 3.4   | 1.3 |

Source: Recascino-Wise and Jonzon, 1990 (taken by them from Statistics Sweden).

Other evidence that the youth-disenfranchisement process is at work in Sweden can be found with wage levels. Over the 1980s, income increases for those between the ages of 16 and 24 did not match the increases of other age groups. For example, in manual occupations, young males earned 82 percent of the average manual worker salary. This decline in earning power can be partly attributed to young people staying in school longer in response to changes in higher educational policy. This includes free tuition and a generous loan and grant system. These changes, along with a housing shortage, have also meant that more Swedish youth live with their parents. In 1985, almost 50 percent of males and 25 percent of females aged 20 to 24 were still living at home. On the other hand, if we compare these figures with those for Canadian youth, we see that the disenfranchisement process has been less severe in Sweden. As noted in chapter 2, in Canada, 70 percent of males and 60 percent of females in this age category were living with their parents in 1986.

So what has the Swedish government done to fight the disenfranchisement processes affecting the young? It certainly has not ignored the problem, or exacerbated it as other countries have done. With widespread popular support, the government immediately took measures to counteract these processes. They may not have been entirely successful, but they have prevented the serious deterioration we are witnessing in Canada and the United States.

As table 6.1 shows, Sweden has come quite close to realizing its goal of full employment. The recession of the early 1980s presented a serious threat to this plan, principally by putting young people out of work (the over-25 age group was only marginally affected as table 6.2 indicates). Responding quickly, the Labor Market Board convinced the government to introduce programs that would make it unnecessary for the unemployed simply to collect benefits. The two principal programs were the Youth Opportunities program, which began in 1980 and targeted those 16 and 17 years of age, and the Youth Teams one, implemented in 1984 mainly for those 18 and 19. Two other minor programs were also introduced during this time. The two major ones provided job counseling, training, and placement. If jobs could not be found in the private sector after a specified period, young people were guaranteed positions in the public sector, mainly with municipal governments. The programs cost the Swedish government about two to three percent of their gross national product a year.[3]

Table 6.3 traces the impact of these programs on the unemployment rate. Evidently these ventures created the buffer needed to help young Swedes ride out the recession. The Youth Teams program seems to have been particularly effective. Note that it was phased out in 1989 when it was no longer needed (after the economic recovery, the youth unemployment rate fell to about three percent, which is actually below the prerecession rate).

Other long-standing policies have benefited young people. One such policy guarantees those who remain students a certain income level. The child allowance, which is paid to parents until their offspring are 16 years old, is converted to a student grant. At 16, the young student is entitled to this

**Table 6.3**

**Labor force status of population aged 16 to 19 years: percentage by category, 1980–1988**

|  | 1980 | 1981 | 1982 | 1983 | 1984 | 1985 | 1986 | 1987 | 1988 |
|---|---|---|---|---|---|---|---|---|---|
| Regular Employment | 89 | 88 | 81 | 75 | 73 | 77 | 79 | 83 | 88 |
| Youth Opportunity Program | 0 | 0 | 2 | 6 | 6 | 5 | 5 | 5 | 4 |
| Youth Teams Program | — | — | — | — | 14 | 14 | 12 | 9 | 0 |
| Unemployed | 8 | 9 | 10 | 11 | 5 | 4 | 4 | 3 | 3 |
| Relief | 3 | 3 | 7 | 8 | 2 | 0 | 0 | 0 | 5 |
|  | 100% | | | | | | | | |

Source: Recascino-Wise and Jonzon, 1990 (taken by them from the Swedish Labor Market Board).

grant and between the ages of 18 and 20 receives it directly. At this point, the other educational grants we alluded to are available. These measures help young people undertake the process of building a life of their own and gain independence from their families.

Another policy that has indirectly protected the young is the goal of full employment and a fair distribution of income.[4] Swedes prefer their citizens to engage in productive labor rather than simply receiving benefits in the form of handouts. The Labor Market Administration is vested with the full-employment mandate, and it coordinates job placements with a network of local offices that constitute the Employment Service System. This system works with local school authorities to help young people through the transition from secondary schools, which emphasize vocational training, into the local labor force. In addition, local school authorities are expected to help students adjust to the workplace.[5]

But there is more to assisting the young than simply guaranteeing them an income. To live fully, they also need to participate in social activities. In this area, as well, Swedes have established an exemplary system. For example, while drug use is rampant among American youth, it declined among Swedish youth between 1977 and 1989 (for instance, in 1977, eight percent of 15-year-olds had used drugs compared to three percent in 1988).[6] Instead of taking drugs as a form of recreation, Swedish youth participate in more meaningful leisure activities, made possible by a compassionate government and adult community. And we use the latter term quite literally, for much of the support for youth activity is at the municipal level. With just over one million citizens aged 16 to 24, there are about 1,600 youth recreational centers in Sweden, 300 of which are nongovernmental organizations. In addition, there are more than 80 youth organizations, funded by the State Youth Council. These organizations have 17,000 local branches that run various programs for young people (and this figure does not include sports clubs). Finally, half of those aged 16 to 25 belong to a trade union.[7]

The impact of these efforts can be seen in the involvement of young people in sociocultural activities. For example, young Swedes are highly musical. One in five 15- to 25-year-olds plays an instrument; one in five females and one in 10 males are active singers; and 25 percent of those between the ages of 10 and 20 attend municipal music classes. Those aged 15 to 24 are actually the most active readers of all age groups in Sweden, spending an average of almost half an hour per day doing so.[8]

These sociocultural activities have contributed to making today's young Swedes a politically aware and socially conscious generation. Surveys indicate that 80 percent of 18- to 21-year-olds voted in the 1988 election;[9] 70 percent of 16- to 25-year-olds regularly discuss politics; and 90 percent would wear a badge to support an organization they believed in and 75 percent would collect money for it. In addition 75 percent would reduce their own standard of living to alleviate environmental problems (50 percent of young people see the environment as the main political issue).

The contrast with youth in many other advanced industrial countries is striking. As we have argued throughout this book, young people in many of these countries have been conditioned into mindless consumerism and unattainable materialism, and some are now taking out their frustrations by engaging in gratuitous violence. The Swedish case demonstrates that when self-development and independent thinking are encouraged, young people will respond positively.

Still, some readers may feel that Swedish social policies are too expensive, that they put too much of a burden on the taxpayer. However, when balanced against the long-term costs of a high crime rate, escalating prison and court courts, and the poor quality of education found in other countries, Swedish policies seem more attractive. The voting public in other countries must learn that they can pay now or they can pay later, but at some point they must pay to maintain their communities and to welcome new generations. If they put it off, many people will suffer needlessly. In contrast, the young are relatively happy in Sweden. Swedes have worked out a compassionate system that is conducive to the psychological well-being of *all* of its citizens and it has a high standard of living. As Stig Hadenius and Ann Lindgren note, "the number of telephones, VCRs, cars, boats, and second homes per person is among the world's highest." With a minimum of five weeks per year paid vacation, even "80% of blue-collar workers can afford an annual vacation trip, and numerous Swedes travel to foreign countries."[10]

Clearly, Sweden's concern for its young has not unduly burdened the taxpayer, and there is no reason that we cannot take a lesson from that nation's exemplary policies.

## RECOMMENDATIONS TO YOUNG PEOPLE

There does not appear to be a political revolution on the horizon that would eradicate the problems facing contemporary youth. On the one hand, advanced industrial societies provide many people with abundant material rewards, making it unlikely that they would support a revolutionary movement of this nature. On the other hand, many of those who are not rewarded in these societies have been so mystified by consent-manufacturing enterprises that they would not know what to fight for or whom to fight against. These mystification enterprises help explain why the signs of dissent we are now witnessing among youth are anarchistic. This dissent is thus unlikely to culminate in a political movement leading them to attempt to overthrow their oppressors.

In this light, *Brave New World* rings true today. For example, the extrinsic reward structure of industrial capitalism has made many people "love their servitude." In this "brave new world," when the pressures get too great, or when the suffering breaks into one's consciousness, people merely escape through mind-altering substances or distracting electronic pursuits. Among the masses, who have been assigned to menial positions with no real hope of improvement, a consensus has been manufactured based on a combination of false hopes, which recalls the lottery system in *Nineteen Eighty-Four*. The masses do not know whom to blame for their troubles except themselves or their families, and they are often led through propaganda efforts (e.g., advertising and televised election campaigns) to support those who act directly against their interests.

So, who do we blame and what do we do about the problems facing young people? First, it is important to recognize that the current state of affairs has slowly evolved over the past century as a result of thousands of individual political and economic decisions. These decisions have been made by individuals in power who act on self-interest and the interests of the groups to which they belong or with which they identify. The groups in question include capitalists, legislators, advertisers, and journalists, but they also include parents, employers, educators, religious leaders, social scientists, and other adult groups that have interests not shared by younger people. We are not arguing that these groups sat down and masterminded a conspiracy against young people. To the contrary, many of those making these decisions thought that they were acting in the best interest of young people. And many of their decisions have been in the interest of young people. However, when these decisions are viewed in their entirety, one has to conclude that numerous unanticipated, negative consequences have resulted from many of them.

Second, in reference to what to do about the plight of the young, the place to begin is with the ideology of youth. As we have argued, the ideology justifying the disenfranchisement of youth is exposed in light of the evidence. For example, technology has deskilled many jobs and made human labor redundant. Only a small proportion of the population is actually needed to maintain the advanced technological component of society. The rest of us are needed to consume the technology mindlessly — to play with it until we tire of it and crave greater sophistication. At the same time, some two-thirds of jobs in advanced industrial societies have not increased in complexity, so there is no use in pretending that everyone must be pushed through a mass educational system to be trained for them. The primary quality needed for many of these jobs is the willingness to conform to the system without questioning it, and the educational system often accomplishes this by breaking the spirit and dulling the minds of young people.

Therefore, we need a revolution in the way we think about youth and coming of age. We must realize, for example, that the ideology of youth is responsible for the identity confusion many young people experience. In many cases, much of this confusion, which may precipitate a crisis, is the product of the social environment of the young. Moreover, most of these young people do not recognize that they are confused and neither do their elders. Rather, their troubles are thought to be natural, the result of an inevitable biological deficiency that passes with age. However, the cause of the identity crisis should be attributed mostly to deficits in the environment, not to shortcomings in the individual.

The wrongheadedness of the ideology of youth becomes apparent if we consider the recommendations made in a recent report concerning the "drop-out problem" in Canada.[11] As discussed in chapter 2, the high-school drop-out rate in many Western countries is considered high. In credentialist societies, this poses a serious problem because career opportunities are based on the number of years of education an individual has accumulated. The solution to the problem outlined in that report was to raise the age one must remain in school from 16 to 18, thereby forcing young people to stay in school longer.[12] From a commonsense point of view, this is reasonable: if people are doing things that are harmful to them, such as dropping-out, then we should stop them.

Unfortunately, this is how we address many social problems. We do not attempt to solve them by getting at their causes, especially when the causes are not obvious or are rooted in the wider social order that the rest of the community benefits from. Rather, we repeatedly apply "Band-Aid solutions," that is, we attempt to mask the problem or treat the symptom rather than the cause. In this case, observers like Ken Dryden, the author of the report, do not attempt to understand why so many students are alienated from the educational system. Instead, Dryden suggests that we force teenagers to endure an experience that many of them find unbearable by raising the age of compulsory school attendance to age 18. But if the system were bearable in the first place, people would remain in it voluntarily.

As we have previously mentioned, these types of solutions place the responsibility for a problem squarely on the shoulders of individuals — *they* must adjust. We leave it to the victim to remedy the problem. This solution ignores the possibility that young people may not be to blame if they do not like being treated as children in high school; if they do not like having their spirit broken by bureaucrats and the agents of bureaucracies (i.e., teachers, guidance counselors, et cetera); or if they do not like being disenfranchised from full participation in the wider society. This type of solution also overlooks the possibility that many young people sense that they have the capacity to be self-directing and mature citizens and that they therefore resent being forced to subject themselves to such an unnatural and alienating environment. Indeed, it ignores the possibility that sometimes the best thing they can do for themselves is to get out of that environment.

In other words, the easy way out is to "adjust" people to their environment and to ignore the possibility of adjusting the environment to people, or to adjust it to suit various individuals. If we alter our way of thinking and follow the Swedish model, for example, we will begin to modify our programs and institutions to suit the needs of young people. In doing so, we would be respecting them as autonomous human beings, and we would also recognize that they do develop special needs as they come of age and join the ranks of adult society.

As we have stressed, in order to help youths, we must focus on the real causes of their problems. And we can do so by adopting the premise that personal troubles, which many people ascribe to an individual's idiosyncratic weaknesses, can often be explained by larger problems within society, as we have argued throughout this book. This insight was developed by C. Wright Mills and forms the basis of what he calls the "sociological imagination."[13]

In addition to thinking along these lines, one needs a vision of what a less alienating society would be like. We believe North American society could be improved if people were to adopt humanistic values that place personal well-being ahead of materialism and a preoccupation with advancing technology. Countries like Canada and the United States emphasize the latter values, although they pretend to be humanistic. Sweden, however, provides a model of a humanistic society, which we would benefit from emulating.

Policies and programs that are informed by humanistic values take into account the experiences and perspectives of those they are ostensibly supposed to benefit. Too many programs become avenues of sinecure for those administering them, and their clientele becomes secondary. Too many programs and institutions operate in their separate and sometimes competitive spheres so that there are great gaps that allow people to "fall through the cracks." Accountability and coordination among such programs can eliminate much of the expense that has given government-sponsored programs a bad name in countries like the United States.

Again, the Swedish experience can provide other countries with a model of effective and rational service delivery. Consequently, rather than simply forcing young people to stay in school until they are 18, programs directed at career counseling, cooperative work-school programs, and job placement could bolster an educational system more rationally integrated with the workplace. Rather than force a large segment of youth into idleness, their energy could be directed in various ways that benefit the national economy, the local community, and themselves.

Finally, young people themselves must take more responsibility for their lives and resist the system's attempts to control and subjudgate them. Moreover, as we have previously mentioned, the young need to realize that if they act irresponsibly or immaturely, they simply confirm negative stereotypes and perpetuate the system that oppresses them. They can also help themselves by realizing that others in their age group are experiencing troubles like their own. It is only by acting collectively to address the social problems that lie at the root of their troubles that they will be able to improve their situation.

By joining forces, young people can oppose the economic controls imposed on them by leading social institutions and gain a say in the policy-making processes that affect them. To ensure that their voice is heard, they should join political youth movements. Once more, Sweden provides a model, with some 115,000 young people belonging to "party political youth organizations" funded by state grants.[14]

As individuals, young people can gain strength by learning about the history of the world in which they live and by becoming aware of the limitations of the institutions governing their lives. With this knowledge, they can direct their own development instead of relying on mass bureaucracies and believing that these bureaucracies will act with their best interests in mind. To gain a better understanding of self-directed development, we recommend that they read *This Book Is Not Required* by Inge Bell.[15]

We laid out some humanistic principles of human development in chapter 3. There we recommended that young people endeavor to tailor their moratorium as much as possible to suit their own needs and help them find and develop their personal strengths. Once developed, the latter can provide a sound basis of ego strength. In addition, the young should remember that while peers can be a positive force in the moratorium, they can also be a negative influence if one depends too heavily on them. The best type of identity moratorium helps one to find one's "real self," not the self others want one to be. Even youths with limited financial resources can find something within themselves or within their immediate communities to which they can commit. Making these commitments can give them a sense of genuinely belonging to the community.

Trite as it may sound, hope for the future lies with new generations, and unless the liabilities plaguing the current generation of young people are rectified, that hope will never be fulfilled. We need to renew our energy and our vision for the future, for it will take energy and vision to turn the tide against the forces oppressing young people as they come of age. Canadians and Americans, both youths and adults, would do well to consider the Swedish coming-of-age model as an alternative to the North American one. Indeed, part of the hype behind their false consciousness is that young people in Canada and the United States are told that they are the most fortunate in the world when, in fact, they are not.

# Notes

## Introduction

1. As cited in M. Lee Manning, "Three Myths Concerning Adolescence," *Adolescence* 18 (1983): 823–29.
2. As cited in John Springhall, *Coming of Age: Adolescence in Britain 1860–1960* (Dublin: Gill and MacMillan, 1986).
3. For a cross-cultural comparison see Margaret Mead, *Coming of Age in Samoa: A Psychological Study of Primitive Youth for Western Civilization* (New York: Morrow Quill Paperbacks, 1928). For a historical analysis see Roy Baumeister and Dianne Tice, "How Adolescence Became the Structure for Self: A Historical Transformation of Psychological Development," in Jerry Suls and Anthony Greenwood, eds., *Psychological Perspectives on the Self*, vol. 3 (Hillsdale, NJ: Lawrence Erlbaum Associates, 1986) 183–201.
4. Lawrence Steinberg, "Pubertal Maturation and Parent-Adolescent Distance: An Evolutionary Perspective," in Gerald Adams, Raymond Montemayor, and Thomas Gullotta, eds., *Biology of Adolescent Behavior and Development* (Beverly Hills, CA: Sage, 1990).
5. G. Stanley Hall, *Adolescence* (New York: Appleton, 1904).
6. An examination of the etymology and meaning of the word *adolescent* suggests that it has negative connotations. The term was coined during the period 1475 to 1485 from the Latin *adolescere*, meaning to grow up. According to the *Random House Webster's Electronic Dictionary*, as an adjective it *now* means "growing into adulthood; youthful . . . characteristic of adolescence; immature," and as a noun it means ". . . a person in the period of adolescence; teenager." In its thesaurus, this dictionary includes the following as synonyms for the adjective: "sophomoric, puerile, pubescent, juvenile; callow, undeveloped; youthful, boyish, girlish; childish, babyish."
7. See, for example, Rolf E. Muuss, *Theories of Adolescence* (New York: McGraw-Hill, 1988).
8. James E. Côté, *Adolescent Storm and Stress: An Evaluation of the Mead/Freeman Controversy* (Hillsdale, NJ: Lawrence Erlbaum,

1994). Briefly, the political implications are that the nature position justifies the status quo — economic and social privilege have a genetic basis in the so-called natural order of things. On the other hand, the nurture position advocates social reform to deal with problems of human societies, because it is believed that societies themselves created the problems with inadequate social environments. For further reading, see William Broad and Nicholas Wade, *Betrayers of the Truth: Fraud and Deceit in the Halls of Science* (New York: Simon and Schuster, 1982).

9. For discussions of Mead's work and the controversy surrounding it, see James E. Côté, "Was Mead Wrong About Coming of Age in Samoa? An Analysis of the Mead/Freeman Controversy for Scholars of Adolescence and Human Development," *Journal of Youth and Adolescence* 21.5 (1992): 1–29; and Côté.

10. Philippe Aries, *Centuries of Childhood* (New York: Random House, 1962); Baumeister and Tice; Marlis Buchmann, *The Script of Life in Modern Society: Entry into Adulthood in a Changing World* (Chicago: University of Chicago Press, 1989); Manning; David Proefrock, "Adolescence: Social Fact and Psychological Concept," *Adolescence* 16 (1981): 851–58.

11. Mead 130–153.

12. Mead 154–162.

13. John R. Gillis, *Youth and History: Tradition and Change in European Age Relations: 1770–Present* (New York: Academic Press, 1974).

## Chapter 1: The Discovery of Youth

1. See Daniel Offer and R. B. Church, "Adolescent Turmoil," in Richard M. Lerner, Anne C. Petersen, and Jeanne Brooks-Gunn, eds., *Encyclopedia of Adolescence* (New York: Garland, 1991) 513–17.

2. See Norman A. Sprinthall and W. Andrew Collins, *Adolescent Psychology: A Developmental View*, 2nd ed. (New York: Random House, 1988) for a detailed history of how the "maturationist" views of Hall and Sigmund Freud evolved into the modern stage-sequence model that is the foundation of contemporary adolescent psychology.

3. Proefrock 851–58.

4. See David Bakan, "Adolescence in America: From Ideas to Social Fact," in C. J. Gaurdo, ed., *The Adolescent as Individual* (New York: Harper and Row, 1975). A "status offense" is an

offense by virtue of one's status as a nonadult — it is not an offense for adults. According to Gerald R. Adams and Thomas P. Gullotta, the authors of *Adolescent Life Experiences* (Pacific Grove, CA: Brooks/Cole, 1989), females and minority group members appear to be charged with these offenses more than white males, suggesting that prejudices come into play.

5.  Gary B. Melton, "Rights of Adolescents," in Lerner, Petersen, and Brooks-Gunn 931.
6.  Proefrock 857–58.
7.  This deficit and other problems in the area of adolescent research have been recently acknowledged by the American Psychological Association; its influential journal *American Psychologist* devoted a full issue to the problem. See especially Richard Jessor, "Successful Adolescent Development among Youth in High-Risk Settings," *American Psychologist*, 48 (1993): 117–126.
8.  D. W. Winnicott, "Adolescence: Struggling through the Doldrums," *Adolescent Psychiatry* 1 (1971): 40–41.
9.  Winnicott 40.
10. Winnicott 41.
11. Dana L. Farnsworth, "Adolescence: Terminable and Interminable," *Adolescent Psychiatry* 3 (1973): 31.
12. Richard F. Hill and J. Dennis Fortenberry, "Adolescence as a Culture-Bound Syndrome," *Social Science and Medicine* 35 (1992): 78. In chapter 2, we review a number of statistical trends regarding the situations confronting young people that support the Hill and Fortenberry critique.
13. Sherman C. Feinstein, "Identity and Adjustment Disorders of Adolescence" in Harold I. Kaplan and Benjamin J. Sadock, eds., *Comprehensive Textbook of Psychiatry*, 4th ed. (Baltimore: Williams and Wilkins, 1985) 1760–65.
14. Warren J. Gadpaille, "Psychiatric Treatment of the Adolescent," in Kaplan and Sadock 1812.
15. See D. L. Rosenhan, "On Being Sane in Insane Places," *Science* 179 (1973): 250–58.
16. Norman A. Sprinthall and W. Andrew Collins, *Adolescent Psychology: A Developmental View* (Reading, MA: Addison-Wesley, 1984) 386.
17. Norman Garmezy, "DSM III. Never Mind the Psychologists: Is It Good for the Children?" *The Clinical Psychologist*, 31 (1983): 4–6.
18. Sprinthall and Collins 386.

19. Feinstein 1765.
20. See Mead.
21. Anne C. Petersen and Brandon Taylor, "The Biological Approach to Adolescence: Biological Change and Psychological Adaptation," in Joseph Adelson, ed., *Handbook of Adolescent Psychology* (New York: John Wiley and Sons, 1980) 117.
22. Jeanne Brooks-Gunn and Michelle P. Warren, "Biological and Social Contributions to Negative Affect in Young Adolescent Girls," *Child Development* 60 (1989) 47.
23. Brooks-Gunn and Warren 47.
24. See Christy Miller Buchanan, Jacquelynne S. Eccles, and Jill B. Becker, "Are Adolescents the Victims of Raging Hormones: Evidence for Activational Effects of Hormones on Moods and Behavior at Adolescence," *Psychological Bulletin* 111 (1992): 62–107; Elizabeth J. Susman and Lorah D. Dorn, "Hormones and Behavior in Adolescence," in Lerner, Petersen, and Brooks-Gunn 513–17; J. Richard Udry, "Adolescent Problem Behavior," *Social Biology* 37 (1990): 1–10.
25. See Roberta L. Paikoff and Jeanne Brooks-Gunn, "Physiological Processes: What Role Do They Play in the Transition to Adolescence?" in Raymond Montemayor, Gerald R. Adams, and Thomas P. Gullotta, eds., *From Childhood to Adolescence: A Transitional Period?* (Beverly Hills, CA: Sage, 1990) 63–81; David C. Rowe and Joseph Lee Rodgers, "Behavioral Genetics, Adolescence Deviance, and 'D': Contributions and Issues," in Adams, Montemayor, and Gullotta 38–67.
26. Marvin Harris argues that genetics has not played a significant role in cultural evolution for many thousands of years, and most certainly not over the past 12,000 years, during which time there has been "an immense diversity of technological, demographic, ecological, economic, sexual, ideological institutions and customs." ("Margaret and the Giant-Killer," *The Sciences* 23 [1983]: 21)
27. Sprinthall and Collins 79.
28. Readers are reminded that when gender or race discrimination is justified on the grounds of an imputed biological inferiority many people get very upset.
29. In this section, we deal only with sociological views of youth partly because the anthropological view is more widely known and partly because the sociological views are more relevant to advanced industrial societies.
30. See Roy F. Baumeister, *Identity: Cultural Change and the*

*Struggle for Self* (New York: Oxford University Press, 1986); Joseph F. Kett, *Rites of Passage* (New York: Basic, 1977).

31. This is referred to as the secular trend. See Sprinthall and Collins 79.

32. Richard Worstal Brunstetter and Larry B. Silver, "Normal Adolescent Development," in Kaplan and Sadock 1608–13.

33. Steinberg 92.

34. There is some disagreement as to how recent economic change should be referred to. Some prefer the term *post industrial*, while others prefer terms like *late capitalism*. We have chosen the term *advanced industrial* because it is widely used. We define the term more precisely in the next chapter.

35. Kenneth Keniston, "Prologue: Youth as a Stage of Life," in Robert J. Havighurst and P. H. Dreyer, eds., *Youth* (Chicago: University of Chicago Press, 1975); Hugh Klein, "Adolescence, Youth, and Young Adulthood: Rethinking Current Conceptualizations of Life Stage," *Youth and Society* 21 (1990): 446–71.

36. Baumeister and Tice 186.

37. Wendell W. Cultice, *Youth's Battle for the Ballot: A History of Voting Age in America* (New York: Greenwood Press, 1992) 3.

38. Anne C. Petersen and Brandon Taylor, "The Biological Approach to Adolescence: Biological Change and Psychological Adaptation," in Joseph Adelson, ed., *Handbook of Adolescent Psychology* (New York: John Wiley and Sons, 1980) 177–155.

39. Raymond Montemayor and Daniel J. Flannery, "Making the Transition from Childhood to Early Adolescence," in Raymond Montemayor, Gerald R. Adams, and Thomas P. Gullotta, eds., *From Childhood to Adolescence: A Transitional Period?* (Beverly Hills, CA: Sage, 1990) 294.

40. Montemayor, Adams, and Gullotta 10.

41. Sprinthall and Collins 2.

42. Sprinthall and Collins 3.

43. This view is derived from symbolic interactionism, a theory based on the premise that interaction is contingent upon our ability to share meanings with each other, particularly on the basis of verbal and nonverbal communication.

44. For a detailed discussion of youth subcultures see Michael Brake, *Comparative Youth Culture: The Sociology of Youth Culture and Youth Subculture in America, Britain and Canada* (London: Routledge and Kegan Paul, 1985).

45. Barry Smart, *Postmodernity* (London: Routledge, 1993).
46. Kenneth J. Gergen, "The Decline of Personality," *Psychology Today* (November/December 1992): 59–63.
47. Richard Tinning and Lindsay Fitzclarence, "Postmodern Youth Culture and the Crisis in Australian Secondary School Physical Education," *Quest* 44 (1992): 287–303.
48. Henry Giroux, *Curriculum Discourse as Postmodern Critical Practice* (Geelong, Victoria: Deakin University Press, 1990).
49. Tinning and Fitzclarence 298.
50. Tinning and Fitzclarence 299.
51. Gord Tait, "Youth, Personhood and 'Practices of the Self': Some New Directions for Youth Research," *Australia and New Zealand Journal of Sociology* 29 (1993): 40–54.
52. Tait 40.
53. Tait 44.
54. Michel Foucault, "Technologies of the Self: A Seminar with Michel Foucault," in Luther Martin, Huck Gutman, and Patrick Hutton, eds., *Technologies of the Self* (Amherst: University of Massachusetts Press, 1988).
55. Pierre Bourdieu, *Outline of Theory of Practice* (Cambridge: Cambridge University Press, 1977).
56. Tait 47. For a similar but more elaborate and positivistic formulation, see Marlis Buchmann, *The Script of Life in Modern Society: Entry into Adulthood in a Changing World* (Chicago: University of Chicago Press, 1989).
57. Mica Nava, *Changing Cultures: Feminism, Youth and Consumerism* (Newbury Park: Sage, 1991) 79–81.
58. See Carlo Mongardini, "The Ideology of Postmodernity," *Theory, Culture and Society* 9 (1992): 55–65.
59. See Kate Millet, *Sexual Politics* (New York: Avon, 1971).
60. Cyril Levitt, *Children of Privilege: Student Revolt in the Sixties* (Toronto: University of Toronto Press, 1984); Herbert Marcuse, *One-Dimensional Man* (Boston: Beacon Press, 1964); Marcuse, *An Essay on Liberation* (Boston: Beacon Press, 1969); Marcuse, *Counter-Revolution and Revolt* (Boston: Beacon Press, 1972); John Rowntree and Margaret Rowntree, "The Political Economy of Youth," *Our Generation* 6 (1968): 155–190.
61. The term "cooling out" was introduced to sociological language by Erving Goffman. This phrase is taken from street language to describe the final phase of a con game during which the person conned (the "mark") is convinced not to go to the authorities, either because he or she will look stupid or

because he or she is culpable. Goffman applied the phrase to a number of institutional spheres in which clients are not fully satisified. See his essay "On Cooling Out the Mark: Some Aspects of Adaptation to Failure," *Psychiatry: Journal for the Study of Interpersonal Relations* 15 (1952): 451–63.

62.  See, for example, Dennis Wrong, "The Over-Socialized Conception of Man in Modern Sociology," *American Sociological Review* 2 (1961): 188–92.

63.  See Derek Freeman, *Margaret Mead and Samoa: The Making and Unmaking of an Anthropological Myth* (Cambridge, MA: Harvard University Press, 1983); and Muuss.

64.  Lawrence Steinberg, "Bound to Bicker," *Psychology Today* (September 1987): 36–39; Steinberg, "Pubertal Maturation."

65.  Baumeister and Tice 187.

66.  See James S. Coleman, *Youth: Transition to Adulthood* (Chicago: University of Chicago Press, 1974).

## Chapter 2: The Liabilities of Youth in Advanced Industrial Society

1.  See David Ashton and Graham Lowe, *Making Their Way: Education, Training and the Labour Market in Canada and Britain* (Toronto: University of Toronto Press, 1991).

2.  Nava 80–83.

3.  E. Ellis Cashmore, *No Future: Youth and Society* (London: Heinemann, 1984).

4.  Jeffrey E. Mirel, "Twentieth-Century America, Adolescence in," in Lerner, Petersen, and Brooks-Gunn 1154.

5.  See, for example, Ivor Berg, *Education and Jobs: The Great Training Robbery* (New York: Praeger Publishers for the Center for Urban Education, 1979); and Randall Collins, *The Credential Society: A Historical Sociology of Education and Stratification* (New York: Academic Press, 1979).

6.  John Porter, "Education and the Just Society," in Alexander Himelfarb and C. James Richardson, eds., *Sociology for Canadians: A Reader* (Toronto: McGraw-Hill Ryerson, 1984).

7.  Berg.

8.  John Myles, "The Expanding Middle: Some Canadian Evidence on the Deskilling Debate," *Canadian Review of Sociology and Anthropology* 25 (1988): 335–364.

9.  Harry Braverman, *Labor and Monopoly Capitalism* (New York: Monthly Review Press, 1974).

10.  Braverman; James Rinehart, *The Tyranny of Work* (Toronto: Academic Press, 1986).

11. The computer has also taken over some management functions — for example, by keeping track of keystroke speed and error rates.

12. Lucie Nobert, Ramona McDowell, and Diana Goulet, *Profile of Higher Education in Canada: 1991 Edition* (Ottawa: Ministry of Supply and Services, 1991) 1.

13. Warren Clark and Z. Zsigmond, *Job Market Reality for Post Secondary Graduates: Employment Outcome by 1978, Two Years After Graduation.* (Ottawa: Ministry of Supply and Services, 1981).

14. Warren Clark, Margaret Laing, and Edith Rechnitzer, *The Class of '82: Summary Report on the Findings of the 1984 National Survey of the Graduates of 1982* (Ottawa: Ministry of Supply and Services, 1986).

15. Gilles Jamsin and Ramona McDowell, *The Labour Market Experience of Social Science Graduates: The Class of 1982 Revisited* (Ottawa: Department of the Secretary of State of Canada, 1989).

16. Nobert, McDowell, and Goulet 41.

17. Max L. Carey, "Occupational Employment Growth Through 1990," *Monthly Labor Review* 104 (1981): 42–55.

18. Daniel E. Hecker, "Reconciling Conflicting Data on Jobs for College Graduates," *Monthly Labor Revew* (July 1992): 4.

19. Kristina J. Shelley, "The Future of Jobs for College Graduates," *Monthly Labor Review* (July 1992): 13–21.

20. Instead, this estimate is based on 29 million workers in the U.S. labor force with four or more years of college education. Even so, with an optimistic projection of moderate employment growth, only about "7 of 10 college graduates joining the labor force" between 1990 and 2005 "can expect to enter jobs requiring a college degree" (Shelley 13).

21. Hecker 7.

22. Compare John Hagan and Blair Wheaton, "The Search for Adolescent Role Exits and the Transition to Adulthood," *Social Forces* 71 (1993): 955–80.

23. Porter 464.

24. Jillian Oderkirk, "Educational Achievement: An International Comparison," *Canadian Social Trends* (Autumn 1993): 8–12.

25. John Myles, G. Picot, and Ted Wannell, *Wages and Jobs in the 1980s: Changing Youth Wages and the Declining Middle* (Ottawa: Statistics Canada, Social and Economic Studies Divison, 1988).

26. Bourdieu.

27. Reginald W. Bibby and Donald C. Posterski, *Teen Trends: A Nation in Motion* (Toronto: Stoddart, 1992) 230.
28. A recent report indicates that in 1988 27.5 percent of Canadian young people between the ages of 18 and 25 were enrolled in university; the figure for the United States was 24.9 percent. This puts both countries in the top three of the OECD countries for university enrollment (Oderkirk).
29. Ken Dryden, *Report of the Ontario Youth Commissioner* (Toronto: Ontario Government, 1986) 14–15.
30. Andy Hargreaves and Ivor Goodson, *Schools of the Future: Towards a Canadian Vision* (Ottawa: Employment and Immigration Canada, 1992) 3. According to a newspaper report by Margaret Polanyi (*Globe and Mail*, September 23, 1988), in Ontario during 1987, the drop-out rates were 20 percent to 25 percent for vocational schools (which largely draw from the working class); 7.5 percent to 12 percent for comprehensive schools; and three to six percent for collegiate institutes (which draw from the middle class and are structured to prepare the individual for university).
31. Hargreaves and Goodson.
32. Deborah Sunter, "School, Work, and Dropping Out," *Perspectives on Labour and Income* (Summer 1993): 44–52. According to this source, an additional 23 percent of this age group were still in high school at the time of the survey.
33. While a 21 percent drop-out rate presents a brighter picture, the authors of the study warn that this rate is for analytic purposes and is only one way to measure the drop-out rate. In this case the rate is based on a self-report survey, which is prone to standard sampling and measurement problems. Another estimate, based on the cohort method of following those who start grade nine, shows a drop-out rate of 32 percent for 1991 (down from 38 percent in 1979), but this does not take into account those who take longer than the standard time to graduate (Sunter 49). Using the same survey results (the School-Leavers Survey conducted by Employment and Immigration Canada) other researchers concluded that only 18 percent of 20-year-olds did not have a high-school diploma (Sid Gilbert and Bruce Orok, "School-leavers," *Canadian Social Trends* (Autumn 1993): 2–7.
34. In comparison with the other OECD countries, Canada is in about the middle in terms of dropouts whereas the United States is among the lowest (Oderkirk).

35. This constitutes a decline of about 50 percent for blacks since 1970 (*Statistical Abstracts of the United States*, U.S. Department of Commerce, 1991, 156).

36. Sid Gilbert, *Attrition in Canadian Universities* (Guelph, ON: Commission of Inquiry on Canadian University Education, 1991).

37. Studies that have tracked Canadian students who discontinue their studies at a particular university have found that about "2–3% . . . are persisters, 10% are academic failures, and 10% represent transfers to other universities and community college." This would reduce the estimate of attrition to about 20 percent of an entering cohort (Gilbert 14).

38. The Canadian figures for postgraduate incompletion are about 30 percent for master's degrees and 50–70 percent for Ph.D.s. In some programs, such as agriculture, women graduate students are up to twice as likely to drop out than men are, but in social science doctoral programs men are more likely to drop out (Gilbert 12).

39. Alan Pomfret, "Education," in James J. Teevan, *Introduction to Sociology: A Canadian Focus* (Scarborough, ON: Prentice-Hall, 1982) 261–89.

40. Hargreaves and Goodson 19.

41. Alexander Lockhart, "Graduate Unemployment and the Myth of Human Capital," in D. T. Davies and K. Herman, eds., *Social Space: Canadian Perspective* (Toronto: New Press, 1971).

42. Jo-Anne B. Parliament, "Labour Force Trends: Two Decades in Review," *Canadian Social Trends* (Autumn 1990): 19.

43. Jeff O'Neill, "Changing Occupational Structure," *Canadian Social Trends* (Winter 1991): 12.

44. Colin Lindsay, "The Service Sector in the 1980s," *Canadian Social Trends* (Spring 1989): 22–23, reports that of those between the ages of 15 and 24 "64% of men and 87% of women had service sector jobs" in 1987.

45. Gary A. Fine, Jeylan T. Mortimer, and Donald F. Roberts, "Leisure, Work, and the Mass Media," in S. Shirley Feldman and Glen R. Elliott, eds., *At the Threshold: The Developing Adolescent* (Cambridge, MA: Harvard University Press, 1990) 238.

46. Myles, Picot, and Wannell 7.

47. Myles, Picot, and Wannell 9.

48. Myles, Picot, and Wannell 97.

49. Compare David W. Livingstone, "Lifelong Education and Chronic Underemployment: Exploring the Contradiction," in Paul Anisef and Paul Axelrod, eds., *Transitions: Schooling and Employment in Canada* (Toronto: Thompson Educational Publishing, 1993).

50. Ted Wannell, "Losing Ground: Wages of Young People, 1981–1986," *Canadian Social Trends* (Summer 1989): 21–22.

51. Myles, Picot, and Wannell 28.

52. Monica Boyd and Ed Pryor, "Young Adults Living in Their Parents' Homes," *Canada Social Trends* (Summer 1989): 17.

53. Boyd and Pryor 19.

54. Harvey Krahn and Graham Lowe, "Transitions to Work: Findings from a Longitudinal Study of High-School and University Graduates in Three Canadian Cities," in David-Ashton and Graham Lowe 164.

55. The William T. Grant Foundation, *The Forgotten Half: Non-College Youth in America* (Washington: William T. Grant Foundation, 1988) 10.

56. Mia Stainby, *Peterborough Examiner* (January 5, 1993): B5.

57. Hargreaves and Goodson 1.

58. Statistics Canada, *Youth in Canada: Selected Highlights* (Ottawa: Housing, Family, and Social Statistics Division, 1989) 32.

59. Michael McCulloch, "The Facts of Employment, 1990," *Perception* (Canadian Council on Social Development) 15 (1991): 17–19.

60. Linda Nielsen, *Adolescence: A Contemporary View*, 2nd ed., (Fort Worth, Texas: Harcourt Brace Jovanovich, 1991).

61. OECD, *Becoming Adult in a Changing Society* (Paris: OECD, 1985).

62. Constance Sorrentino, "International Comparisons of Unemployment Indicators," *Monthly Labor Review* (March 1993): 3–15.

63. According to Mary Sue Devereaux, to be counted as officially unemployed in Canada, "a person must not have worked in the reference week; must have actively sought work sometime in the previous four weeks; and, must be currently available to take a job." ("Alternative Measures of Unemployment," *Perspectives on Labour and Income* [Winter 1992]: 36).

64. Discouraged workers are those who have given up looking for a job because they do not believe any suitable positions are available. See Devereaux.

65. Akyeampong reports figures that indicate that the number of discouraged workers aged 15 to 24 decreased from 57,000 in 1983 to 19,000 in 1992 ("Discouraged Workers — Where Have They Gone?" *Perspectives on Labour and Income* [Autumn 1992]: 38–44. Not coincidentally, over the same time postsecondary enrollments increased by about 200,000 [See also Nobert, McDowell, and Goulet]).

66. "Jobless Rate Edges Down, But . . ." *London Free Press* (September 11, 1993): B14.

67. David P. Ross and Richard Shillington, *The Canadian Fact Book on Poverty, 1989* (Ottawa: Canadian Council on Social Development, 1990) 93.

68. *The Forgotten Half* 20.

69. Comparisons among countries are inexact because different definitions of poverty are often used.

70. Steven E. Haugen and Earl F. Mellor, "Estimating the Number of Minimum Wage Earners," *Monthly Labor Review* (January 1990): 70–74.

71. Marshall Korenblum, "Canada's Troubled Youth and the Real Victim of Society?" *Globe and Mail* (March 24, 1986): A7.

72. Statistics Canada, *Health Reports* (Ottawa: Canadian Centre for Health Information, 1989).

73. David A. Cole, "Adolescent Suicide," in Lerner, Petersen, and Brooks-Gunn; David K. Curran, *Adolescent Suicidal Behavior* (New York: Hemisphere Publishing, 1987).

74. Cole.

75. Renée Beneteau, "Trends in Suicide," *Canadian Social Trends* (Winter 1988): 22–24.

76. Curran.

77. Cole.

78. Beneteau.

79. Recently, public attention in Canada has been directed by the media to the high suicide rate among young native Canadians living in isolated communities in the Arctic. This was prompted by a group suicide attempt in one such community, Davis Inlet.

80. Nielsen.

81. Cole.

82. Nielsen.

83. Nielsen.

84. Scott P. Strang and Jacob L. Orlofsky, "Factors Underlying Suicidal Ideation Among College Students: A Test of Teicher and Jacob's Model," *Journal of Adolescence* 13 (1990): 39–52.

85. Cole 1113.
86. Daniel Offer and Melvin Sabshin, *Normality and the Life Cycle: A Critical Integration* (New York: Basic Books, 1984) 101.
87. Offer and Sapshin 92–94.
88. Martin Seligman, "Boomer Blues," *Psychology Today* October 1988: 50–55.
89. Statistics Canada, *Health Reports.*
90. Jeffrey Arnett, "Reckless Behavior in Adolescence: A Developmental Perspective," *Developmental Review* 12 (1992): 339–373.
91. Arnett.
92. Barbara Kantrowitz, "Wild in the Streets," *Newsweek* (August 2, 1993): 40–47.
93. Nielsen.
94. Nielsen.
95. Kantrowitz.
96. Neil Howe and Bill Strauss, *13th GEN: Abort, Retry, Ignore, Fail?* (New York: Vintage Books, 1993) 121.
97. The recent film *Boyz-n-the-Hood* portrays many of the problems facing the young black male growing up in urban America.
98. Gary B. Melton, "Rights of Adolescents," in Lerner, Petersen, and Brooks-Gunn 930.
99. Kathleen Cawsey, "Fifth Column: Personals," *Globe and Mail* (April 12, 1993): A10.
100. As people become established in their careers, they are able to consolidate their positions in the form of higher incomes, greater bank savings, bigger houses, and more expensive cars. They feel they deserve these trappings of success not necessarily because they have become more productive or because they are making significant contributions to the economy, but rather simply because they are getting older. While this is a widely accepted practice, it is a form of ageism that undermines opportunities for the young.
101. Wannell 21.
102. In the United States, the segment of the population aged 15 to 24 is also shrinking. "Between 1980 and 1996 [it] . . . is expected to fall 21 percent, from about 43 to 34 million" (William T. Grant Foundation 9). This constitutes a decline from 18.8 percent of the population to 13 percent of the population.
103. Aldous Huxley, *Brave New World* (London: Triad Grafton, 1932/1948) 14.
104. Huxley 13.

105. See Stuart Ewen, *Captains of Consciousness: Advertising and the Social Roots of the Consumer Culture* (New York: McGraw-Hill, 1976) for an analysis of the growth of advertising in the 20th century and its manipulation of consumers' self-image to create the need for consumer products.

## Chapter 3: The Conquest of Youth

1.  James E. Côté, "Foundations of a Psychoanalytic Social Psychology: Neo-Eriksonian Propositions Regarding the Relationship between Psychic Structure and Cultural Institutions," *Developmental Review* 13 (1993): 31–53.
2.  James E. Côté, "Identity Crisis Modality: A Technique for Assessing the Structure of the Identity Crisis," *Journal of Adolescence* 9 (1986): 321–35; Erik H. Erikson, *Identity: Youth and Crisis* (New York: Norton, 1968).
3.  For a treatment of this issue as it applies to 186 preindustrial societies, see Alice Schlegel and Herbert Barry III, *Adolescence: An Anthropological Inquiry* (New York: Free Press, 1991).
4.  Paul Roazen, *Erik H. Erikson: The Power and Limits of a Vision* (New York: Free Press, 1976).
5.  The eight stages are: trust versus mistrust; autonomy versus shame and doubt; initiative versus guilt; industry versus inferiority; identity versus identity confusion; intimacy versus isolation; generativity versus stagnation; and integrity versus despair.
6.  Erikson 17.
7.  James E. Côté and Charles Levine, "A Formulation of Erikson's Theory of Ego Identity Formation," *Developmental Review* 7 (1987): 273–325.
8.  See Saul Levine's, *Radical Departures: Desperate Detours to Growing Up* (New York: Harcourt Brace Jovanovich, 1984) in which he discusses the therapeutic value of cult membership for those who are unable to make a break from their family.
9.  Erik H. Erikson and Kai T. Erikson, "On the Confirmation of the Delinquent," *Chicago Review* 10 (1957): 15–23.
10. See Côté (1994) for an analysis of similar circumstances faced by young people in the "least developed" country of Western Samoa. There it appears that a disjuncture in the continuity of generations, engendered by contact with the West, has left young people alienated from the culture of their parents but unable to embrace Western culture.

11. David Ross, "Action Needed on Education for Indians," *Perception: Canada's Social Development Magazine* (Fall/Winter, 1992): 27–30.
12. Ross.
13. Geoffrey York, "Crime Is Ticket to Escape Northern Woes," *Globe and Mail*, (October 26, 1987): A1, A4.
14. York.
15. William Glasser, *The Identity Society* (New York: Harper and Row, 1972).
16. See Arnett; Richard Jessor, "Risk Behaviour in Adolescence: A Psychosocial Framework for Understanding and Action," *Journal of Adolescent Health* 12 (1991): 597–605.
17. See Erikson; Robert J. Lifton, "Protean Man," *Partisan Review* 35 (1968): 13-27.
18. In the past 20 years, the term *gender* has come into usage to convey the idea that much behavior results from social role allocation. The term *sex* is thought to overemphasize biology as a cause of male-female behavior differences.
19. See Nava.
20. Susan A. Basow, *Gender: Stereotypes and Roles* (Pacific Grove, CA: Brooks/Cole, 1992); Patricia Madoo Lengermann and Ruth A. Wallace, *Gender in America: Social Control and Social Change* (Englewood Cliffs, NJ: Prentice-Hall, 1985); Marlene Mackie, *Gender Relations in Canada: Further Explorations* (Toronto: Butterworths, 1991).
21. In statistical terms, studies show that on average sex explains one percent of the variance in math test scores; on measures of aggression the difference is only six percent (Mackie).
22. Mackie 41; and see table 2.2 in chapter 2.
23. Rachel T. Hare-Mustin and Jeanne Marecek, "The Meaning of Difference: Gender Theory, Postmodernism, and Psychology," *American Psychologist* 43 (1988): 455–64.
24. See Huston and Alvarez.
25. See Nancy Mandell and Stewart Crysdale, "Gender Tracks: Male-Female Perceptions of Home-School-Work Transitions," in Anisef and Axelrod, for a similar conceptualization based on the notion of "gender tracking." In their study, they attempt to tackle the notion of agency through interviews designed to detect how young people experience, conform to, or resist the attempts to "gender track" them.
26. See Elizabeth Douvan and Joseph Adelson, *The Adolescent Experience* (New York: John Wiley, 1966).

27. See Judith A. DiIorio, "Sex, Glorious Sex: The Social Construction of Masculine Sexuality in a Youth Group," in Laurel Richardson and Verta Taylor, eds., *Feminist Frontiers II* (New York: Random House, 1989); Clyde W. Franklin, "The Male Sex Drive," in Richardson and Taylor; Peter Lyman, "The Fraternal Bond as a Joking Relationship: A Case Study of the Role of Sexist Jokes in Male Group Bonding," in Michael S. Kimmel, ed., *Changing Men* (Beverly Hills, CA: Sage, 1987).

28. Douvan and Adelson.

29. See a study that found empirical support for gender intensification in early adolescence but showed that pubertal timing was not related to it: Nancy L. Galambos, David M. Almeida, and Anne C. Petersen, "Masculinity, Femininity, and Sex Role Attitudes in Early Adolescence: Exploring Gender Intensification," *Child Development* 61 (1990): 1905–14.

30. Nielsen 198–99.

31. Huston and Alvarez.

32. Victor Dwyer, "Eye of the Beholder: Young Women Have Self-Image Difficulties," *Maclean's* (February 22, 1993): 46–47; John P. Hill and Mary Ellen Lynch, "The Intensification of Gender-Related Role Expectations During Early Adolescence," in Jeanne Brooks-Gunn and Anne C. Petersen, eds., *Girls at Puberty: Biological and Psychological Perspectives* (New York: Plenum, 1983); Janelle Holmes and Eliane Leslau Silverman, *We're Here, Listen to Us! A Survey of Young Women in Canada* (Ottawa: Canadian Advisory Council on the Status of Women, 1992).

33. Nielsen.

34. Jean Stockard and Miriam M. Johnson, *Sex and Gender in Society* (Englewood Cliffs, NJ: Prentice Hall, 1992).

35. I. Broverman, D. M. Broverman, F. E. Clarson, P. S. Rosenkrantz, and S. R. Vogel, "Sex-Role Stereotypes and Clinical Judgments of Mental Health," *Journal of Consulting and Clinical Psychology* 34 (1970): 1–7; Basow.

36. See Sandra L. Bem and Daryl J. Bem, "Homogenizing the American Woman: The Power of an Unconscious Ideology," in Daryl J. Bem, ed., *Beliefs, Attitudes, and Human Affairs* (Belmont, CA: Brooks/Cole, 1970).

37. Nielsen 195.

38. Nielsen 197.

39. While much of the evidence in this chapter is taken from studies conducted in the United States, we believe it can also

be applied to Canada (see Mackie) and to most other advanced industrial societies.

40. Paul Chance, "Where Have All the Smart Girls Gone?" *Psychology Today* (April 1989): 20.
41. See Renzetti and Curran; Nielsen.
42. Renzetti and Curran 88.
43. Renzetti and Curran 88.
44. Mirra Sadker and David Sadker, "Sexism in the Classroom in the 1980s," *Psychology Today* (March 1985): 54–57.
45. Nielsen 191.
46. Aletha C. Huston and Mildred M. Alvarez, "The Socialization Context of Gender Role Development in Early Adolescence," in Adams, Montemayor, and Gullotta.
47. Renzetti and Curran 86.
48. Renzetti and Curran 85.
49. Stockard and Johnson.
50. Ellis D. Evans, Judith Rutberg, Carmela Sather, and Charlie Turner, "Context Analysis of Contemporary Teen Magazines for Adolescent Females," *Youth and Society* 23 (1991): 99–120.
51. Evans, et al., 110.
52. This term was coined by Marjorie Ferguson in *Forever Feminine: Women's Magazines and the Cult of Femininity* (London: Heinemann, 1983).
53. See Ewen.
54. Thomas R. Forrest, "Such a Handsome Face: Advertising Male Cosmetics," in Richardson and Taylor.
55. Huston and Alvarez.
56. Davis.
57. Davis 330–31.
58. Huston and Alvarez.
59. Huston and Alvarez 172.
60. Basow 162.
61. Huston and Alvarez 173.
62. Basow 165.
63. Kimmel, 1987; M. Messner, "The Life of a Man's Seasons: Male Identity in the Life Course of the Jock," in Kimmel.
64. See Linda L. Lindsey, *Gender Roles: A Sociological Perspective* (Englewood Cliffs, NJ: Prentice-Hall, 1990) 159.
65. Marie Richmond-Abbott, *Masculine and Feminine: Gender Roles Over the Life Cycle* (New York: McGraw-Hill, 1992) 121. The norms of masculinity vary by class but apparently by degree, not kind. Richmond-Abbott summarizes some of this

variation: "The pressure to be tough is greatly intensified for working-class and lower-class boys. Because these boys will probably not compete as much for academic and occupational success as middle-class boys do, toughness is the primary field of competition aside from competition for women. Working-class and lower-class boys are likely to engage in many more fights than their middle-class peers do" (122).

66. See Dwyer.
67. Nielsen 197.
68. Nielsen 198.
69. DiIorio; Lyman.
70. Nielsen 199.
71. From Warren T. Farrell. *The Liberated Man* (New York: Random House, 1974) 224.
72. James E. Côté, "Traditionalism and Feminism: A Typology of Strategies Used by University Women to Manage Career-Family Conflicts," *Social Behaviour and Personality* 14 (1986): 133–43; Mirra Komarovsky, *Dilemmas of Masculinity* (New York: Norton, 1976).
73. Mackie.
74. Joan Z. Spade and Carole A. Reese, "We've Come a Long Way, Maybe: College Students' Plans for Work and Family," *Sex Roles* 24 (1991): 309–321.
75. See, for example, James E. Marcia, "Identity in Adolescence," in J. Adelson, ed., *Handbook of Adolescent Psychology* (New York: Wiley, 1980); Côté.
76. See Marcia; Stockard and Johnson.
77. These figures are based on 1986 data cited by Owen Adams and Dhruva Nagnur, "Marrying and Divorcing: A Status Report for Canada," *Canadian Social Trends* (Summer 1989): 24–27. According to Jean Dumas and Yolande LaVoie, *Report on the Demographic Situation in Canada 1992* (Ottawa: Ministry of Industry, Science, and Technology, 1992), in 1991 78.5 percent of Canadian women between the ages of 20 and 24 were single, compared with only 43.5 percent in 1971. The comparable figures for young men are 91 percent versus 67.6 percent.
78. Mackie.
79. Basow.
80. Linda G. Sexton, *Between Two Worlds: Young Women in Crisis* (New York: Morrow, 1979).
81. Stockard and Johnson.

82. Basow 330.
83. Mackie 259, emphasis in original.
84. Mackie 260.
85. Basow 332.
86. Basow 322.
87. Basow 332.

## Chapter 4: Ideology and the Politics of Social Control

1. Edward S. Herman and Noam Chomsky, *Manufacturing Consent: The Political Economy of the Mass Media* (New York: Pantheon, 1988).
2. Helen Caldicott, *If You Love This Planet: A Plan to Heal the Earth* (New York: Norton, 1992).
3. Edward Bernays, *The Engineering of Consent* (Norman, OK: University of Oklahoma Press, 1955).
4. Caldicott.
5. Mostafa Rejai, "Political Ideology: Theoretical and Comparative Perspectives," in Mostafa Rejai, ed., *Decline of Ideology* (Chicago: Aldine and Atherton, 1971) 3.
6. Gustav Bergman, "Ideology," *Ethics* 61 (April 1951): 210.
7. Garvin McCain and Erwin M. Segal, *The Game of Science* (Belmont, CA: Brooks/Cole, 1969) 31–32.
8. To the extent that language is ideological, we must also realize that ways of seeing are simultaneously ways of not seeing. For in illuminating certain aspects of social reality, language also obscures others by directing our attention away from them.
9. See Allahar 35–37 for a discussion of the labor theory of value and exploitation that is relevant to this issue of profits and cheap labor.
10. Karl Marx and Friedrich Engels, *The German Ideology* (New York: International Publishers, 1969) 39.
11. Frantz Fanon, *The Wretched of the Earth* (New York: Grove Press, 1963) 52.
12. It is worth pointing out that as a result of the recent riots in Los Angeles members of these two gangs came together, made a truce, and agreed that their problems were not really with one another, but rather were systemic. They agreed that their immediate problems were related to racism, economic deprivation, and social exclusion. They identified the predominantly white police force, which was acting on behalf of the government and leading economic interests,

as the prime enemy on which they were going to focus. Unhappily, however, the truce was very short-lived.

13. Lawrence Graham and Lawrence Hamdan, *Youthtrends: Capturing the $200 Billion Youth Market* (Toronto: McClelland and Stewart, 1989).
14. Jo Marney, "Teen Market Offers Growing Opportunities," *Marketing* (December 9, 1991): 14.
15. Collins.
16. Bruce Curtis, *Building the Educational State: Canada West, 1836–1871* (London, ON: Althouse Press, 1988).
17. Collins 5.
18. See Curtis.
19. Collins.
20. Collins 111–12.
21. Collins 117–18.
22. See Bowles and Gintis.
23. Collins 121.
24. Collins 123.
25. Collins 127–28.
26. Collins 17–18.
27. Table 2.1 presented statistics that trace the increases in enrollment achieved over the past century.
28. See Livingstone for an account of higher education and the contradictions of capitalism.
29. Stacey Gibson, "University Degree May Lead to a Dead-End Job: Fill Out That Becker's Application Now Because That's Where an Honours Degree May Get You," *The* [UWO] *Gazette* (March 25, 1993): 1.

## Chapter 5: Complementarity and the Social Control of Dissent

1. George Orwell, *Nineteen Eighty-Four* (New York: Penguin, 1948) 153.
2. Huxley 12.
3. Huxley 12.
4. Huxley 12.
5. Bernd Baldus, "The Study of Power: Suggestions for an Alternative," *Canadian Journal of Sociology* 1 (1975): 179–201; Baldus, "Social Control in Capitalist Societies: An Examination of the Problem of Order in Liberal Democracies," *Canadian Journal of Sociology* 2 (1977): 37–53.
6. See Aldous Huxley, *Brave New World Revisited* (New York: Harper and Row, 1958).

7. Philip Agee, *Inside the Company: The CIA Diary* (Harmondsworth, Eng.: Penguin, 1975).
8. Baldus 250–51.
9. Orwell 82.
10. In the United States, only about 20 percent of 18- to 20-year-olds vote in congressional elections, while only about one-third of this age group vote in presidential elections (versus about 45 percent and 60 percent of the entire voting age population, respectively; Cultice).
11. Kenneth C. Green and Alexander W. Astin, "The Mood on Campus: More Conservative or Just More Materialistic?" *Educational Record* (Winter 1985): 45.
12. Green and Astin 48.
13. Fine, Mortimer, and Roberts.
14. Fine, Mortimer, and Roberts 237–38.
15. Fine, Mortimer, and Roberts 232.
16. Tinning and Fitzclarence 299; see also Gergen.
17. Hargreaves and Goodson 23.
18. Orwell 82.
19. Hargreaves and Goodson 5.
20. See also Canadian Press, "The Economic Council of Canada Says We Pay Out Too Much on Schooling and Get Too Little in Return," *London Free Press* (May 9, 1990): A1.
21. "Education Experiment Is Paying Dividends," *Globe and Mail* (June 3, 1992): A1.
22. One often hears stories of individuals on welfare and others with minimal incomes who spend hundreds of dollars a month on lottery tickets, and thus incur huge debts that can ruin their lives.
23. Donald Sabo and Sue Curry Jansen, "Images of Men in Sport Media: The Social Reproduction of Gender Order," in Steve Craig, ed., *Men, Masculinity, and the Media* (Newbury Park, CA: Sage, 1992) 182–83.
24. Bibby and Posterski.
25. Lynne Ainsworth, "Educators Reject Guards for Schools," *Toronto Star* (May 12, 1991): A1.
26. Bladus 251.
27. Orwell 65.
28. Muzafer Sherif, O. J. Harvey, B. J. White, W. R. Hood, and C. W. Sherif, *Intergroup Conflicted Co-operation: The Robber's Cave Experiment* (Norman, OK: University of Oklahoma, Norman Institute of Group Relations, 1961).

29. It is also relevant to note how, around the same time, the triumph of the Argentine national soccer team at the World Cup competition served to unite this traumatized nation in spirit and fervor. When Argentina won the final game and their heroes returned home in triumph, young and old, rich and poor, free and imprisoned, oppressors and oppressed joined in a rare show of national solidarity that titillated political commentators on both the left and the right.
30. Orwell 66.
31. The historical record will, in fact, show that in the past the United States has only respected the authority of the United Nations when the latter organization was prepared to do its bidding.
32. That Kuwait was not a democracy even before Iraq invaded it did not seem to matter to the United States. Indeed, after the war ended the traditional undemocratic regime was restored and all talk of making the world safe for democracy ended. In the election that was eventually held in Kuwait, only about one in six members of the population — principally wealthy males — was franchised to vote.
33. The irony, however, escaped the main gaze of the bulk of the population, black and white, whose false consciousness led them to think that Iraq was planning to take over the world, just as earlier they were led to believe that if the Sandinistas in Nicaragua were not stopped, they would invade the United States. This is like the psychological and emotional manipulation that became so commonplace in Oceania.
34. Basow 166.
35. See Ewen; Herman and Chomsky.
36. Countless examples of media manipulation of the young could be cited. For a thorough analysis of this problem, we recommend: Quentin J. Schultze, Roy M. Anker, James D. Bratt, William D. Romanowski, John William Worst, and Lambert Zuidervaart, *Dancing in the Dark: Youth, Popular Culture, and the Electronic Media* (Grand Rapids, MI: William B. Eerdmans Publishing, 1990).

## Chapter 6: Toward a New Reality For Youth

1. See Myles, Picot, and Wannell; O'Neill.
2. Unless otherwise indicated, statistics are taken from the following publications obtained from the Swedish Institute: *Fact and Figures About Swedish Youth* (Stockholm, 1991) and *Higher*

*Education in Sweden* (Stockholm, 1992).

3.  Lois Recascino-Wise and Bjorn Jonzon, "Policies for Employing Young People," *Current Sweden No. 371* (Stockholm: Swedish Institute, 1990).

4.  Stig Hadenius and Ann Lindgren, *On Sweden* (Stockholm: Swedish Institute, 1990).

5.  Recascino-Wise and Jonzon.

6.  This compares with a rate of about 14 percent for Canadian youth of the same age (Marc Eliany, "Alcohol and Drug Use," *Canadian Social Trends* [Spring 1991]: 19–26). Note that there was a drop in the Canadian rate, as well, from 32 percent in Canada in 1979.

7.  All figures are from the Swedish Institute.

8.  According to Nielsen, only 35 percent of 17-year-old American males and 45 percent of females can read at an "adept" level (these figures are as low as 20 percent for African-American and Hispanic youths). In Canada, only one in three teenagers engage in "optimal" reading, compared with one in two adults. Instead, most watch TV (90 percent watch it "very often") or listen to their stereo (57 percent do so "very often" [Bibby and Posterski]).

9.  The comparable figure is about 33 percent in the United States for the 1988 election (Cultice).

10. Hadenius and Lindgren 74–75.

11. Note that dropping out of school is now defined as a "problem," to which an army of professionals has been assigned. It is deemed a problem because there is a consensus that people ought to stay in school until they graduate. At the turn of the century, however, this attitude did not exist. That 90 percent of the population did not attend high school but instead worked (see table 2.1) was viewed as normal.

12. Dryden.

13. C. Wright Mills, *The Sociological Imagination* (New York: Oxford University Press, 1959).

14. Swedish Institute.

15. Inge Bell, *This Book Is Not Required* (Fort Bragg, CA: The Small Press, 1985).

# Bibliography

Adams, Gerald R., and Thomas P. Gullotta. *Adolescent Life Experiences*. 2nd ed. Pacific Grove, CA: Brooks/Cole, 1989.

Adams, Owen, and Dhruva Nagnur. "Marrying and Divorcing: A Status Report for Canada." *Canadian Social Trends* (Summer 1989): 23–27.

Agee, Philip. *Inside the Company: The CIA Diary*. Harmondsworth, Eng.: Penguin, 1975.

Ainsworth, Lynne. "Educators Reject Guards for Schools." *Toronto Star* (May 12, 1991): A1.

Akyeampong, Ernest B. "Discouraged Workers — Where Have They Gone?" *Perspectives on Labour and Income* (Autumn 1992): 38–44.

Allahar, Anton L. *Sociology and the Periphery*. Toronto: Garamond Press, 1989.

Aries, Philippe. *Centuries of Childhood*. New York: Random House, 1962.

Arnett, Jeffrey. "Reckless Behavior in Adolescence: A Developmental Perspective." *Developmental Review* 12 (1992): 339–73.

Ashton, David, and Graham Lowe. *Making Their Way: Education, Training and the Labour Market in Canada and Britain*. Toronto: University of Toronto Press, 1991.

Bakan, David. "Adolescence in America: From Ideas to Social Fact." *The Adolescent as Individual*. Ed. C. J. Gaurdo. New York: Harper and Row, 1975.

Baldus, Bernd. "The Study of Power: Suggestions for an Alternative." *Canadian Journal of Sociology* 1 (1975): 179–201. "Social Control in Capitalist Societies: An Examination of the Problem of Order in Liberal Democracies." *Canadian Journal of Sociology* 2 (1977): 37–52.

Basow, Susan A. *Gender: Stereotypes and Roles*. 2nd ed. Pacific Grove, CA: Brooks/Cole, 1992.

Baumeister, Roy F., and Dianne M. Tice. "How Adolescence Became the Struggle for Self: A Historicial Transformation of Psychological Development." *Psychological Perspectives on the Self* 3. Eds. Jerry Suls and Anthony G. Greenwood. Hillsdale, NJ: Lawrence Erlbaum Associates, 1986.

Bell, Inge. *This Book Is Not Required*. Fort Bragg, CA: The Small Press, 1985.

Bem, Sandra L., and Daryl J. Bem. "Homogenizing the American Woman: The Power of an Unconscious Ideology." *Beliefs, Attitudes, and Human Affairs*. Ed. Daryl Bem. Belmont, CA: Brooks/Cole, 1970.

Beneteau, Renée. "Trends in Suicide." *Canadian Social Trends* (Winter 1988): 22–24.

Berg, Ivor. *Education and Jobs: The Great Training Robbery*. New York: Praeger Publishers for the Center for Urban Education, 1970.

Bergman, Gustav. "Ideology." *Ethics* 61 (April 1951): 210.

Bernays, Edward. *The Engineering of Consent*. Norman, OK: University of Oklahoma Press, 1955.

Bibby, Reginald W., and Donald C. Posterski. *Teen Trends: A Nation in Motion*. Toronto: Stoddart, 1992.

Bourdieu, Pierre. *Outline of Theory of Practice*. Cambridge: Cambridge University Press, 1977.

Bowles, Samuel, and Herbert Gintis. *Schooling in Capitalist America*. New York: Basic, 1976.

Boyd, Monica, and Ed Pryor. "Young Adults Living in Their Parents' Homes." *Canadian Social Trends* (1989): 17–20.

Brake, Michael. *Comparative Youth Culture: The Sociology of Youth Culture and Youth Subculture in America, Britain and Canada*. London: Routledge and Kegan Paul, 1985.

Braverman, Harry. *Labour and Monopoly Capitalism*. New York: Monthly Review Press, 1974.

Broad, William, and Nicholas Wade. *Betrayers of the Truth: Fraud and Deceit in the Halls of Science*. New York: Simon and Schuster, 1982.

Brooks-Gunn, Jeanne, and Michelle P. Warren. "Biological and Social Contributions to Negative Affect in Young Adolescent Girls." *Child Development* 60 (1989): 40–55.

Broverman, I., D. M. Broverman, F. E. Clarson, et al. "Sex-Role Stereotypes and Clinical Judgments of Mental Health." *Journal of Consulting and Clinical Psychology* 34 (1970): 1–7.

Brunstetter, Richard Worstal, and Larry B. Silver. "Normal Adolescent Development." *Comprehensive Textbook of Psychiatry*. Eds. Harold I. Kaplan and Benjamin J. Sadock. 4th ed. Baltimore: Williams and Wilkins, 1985.

Buchanan, Christy M., Jacquelynne S. Eccles and Jill B. Becker. "Are Adolescents the Victims of Raging Hormones: Evidence for Activational Effects of Hormones on Moods and Behavior at Adolescence." *Psychological Bullet III* (1992): 62–107.

Buchmann, Marlis. *The Script of Life in Modern Society: Entry into Adulthood in a Changing World*. Chicago: University of Chicago Press, 1989.

Caldicott, Helen. *If You Love This Planet: A Plan to Heal the Earth*. New York: Norton, 1992.

Carey, Max L. "Occupational Employment Growth Through 1990." *Monthly Labor Review* (August 1981): 42–55.

Cashmore, E. Ellis. *No Future: Youth and Society*. London: Heinemann, 1984.

Cawsey, Kathleen. "Kathleen Cawsey Wonders Why Society Discriminates Against Teen-agers." *Globe and Mail* (April 12, 1993): A10.

Chance, Paul. "Where Have All the Smart Girls Gone?" *Psychology Today* (April 1989): 20.

Clark, Warren, Margaret Laing and Edith Rechnitzer. *The Class of '82: Summary Report on the Findings of the 1984 National Survey of the Graduates of 1982*. Ottawa: Ministry of Supply and Services, 1986.

Clark, Warren, and Z. Zsigmond. *Job Market Reality for Post Secondary Graduates. Employment Outcome by 1978, Two Years After Graduation*. Government Catalogue 82-572. Ottawa: Ministry of Supply and Services, 1981.

Cole, David A. "Adolescent Suicide." *Encyclopedia of Adolescence*, 1113–1116. Eds. Richard M. Lerner, Anne C. Petersen, and Jeanne Brooks-Gunn. New York: Garland, 1991.

Coleman, James. *Youth: Transition to Adulthood*. Chicago: University of Chicago Press, 1974.

Collins, Randall. *The Credential Society: A Historical Sociology of Education and Stratification*. New York: Academic Press, 1979.

Côté, James E. "Identity Crisis Modality: A Technique for Assessing the Structure of the Identity Crisis." *Journal of Adolescence* 9 (1986a): 321–35.

————. "Traditionalism and Feminism: A Typology of Strategies Used by University Women to Manage Career-Family Conflicts." *Social Behavior and Personality* 14 (1986b): 133–43.

————. "Was Mead Wrong About Coming of Age in Samoa? An Analysis of The Mead/Freeman Controversy for Scholars of Adolescence and Human Development." *Journal of Youth and Adolescence* 21 (5) (1992): 1–29.

————. "Foundations of a Psychoanalytic Social Psychology: Neo-Eriksonian Propositions Regarding the Relationship Between Psychic Structure and Cultural Institutions." *Developmental Review* 13 (1993): 31–53.

————. *Adolescent Storm and Stress: An Evaluation of the Mead/Freeman Controversy*. Hillsdale, NJ: Lawrence Erlbaum, 1994.

Côté, James E., and Charles Levine. "A Formulation of Erikson's Theory of Ego Identity Formation." *Developmental Review* 7 (1987): 273–325.

Cultice, Wendell W. *Youth's Battle for the Ballot: A History of Voting Age in America*. New York: Greenwood Press, 1992.

Curran, David K. *Adolescent Suicidal Behavior*. New York: Hemisphere Publishing Corporation, 1987.

Curtis, Bruce. *Building the Educational State: Canada West, 1836–1871*. London, ON: Althouse Press, 1988.

Devereaux, Mary Sue. "Alternative Measures of Unemployment." *Perspectives on Labour and Income* (Winter 1992): 35–43.

DiIorio, Judith A. "Sex, Glorious Sex: The Social Construction of Masculine Sexuality in a Youth Group." *Feminist Frontiers II*. Eds. Laurel Richardson and Verta Taylor. New York: Random House, 1989.

Douvan, Elizabeth, and Joseph Adelson. *The Adolescent Experience*. New York: John Wiley, 1966.

Dryden, Ken. *Report of the Ontario Youth Commissioner*. Toronto: Ontario Government, 1986.

Dumas, Jean, and Yolande Lavoie. *Report on the Demographic Situation in Canada 1992*. Ottawa: Ministry of Industry, Science, and Technology, 1992.

Dwyer, Victor. "Eye of the Beholder: Young Women Have Self-Image Difficulties." *Maclean's* (February 22, 1993): 46–47.

Eliany, Marc. "Alcohol and Drug Use." *Canadian Social Trends* (Spring 1991): 19–26.

Erikson, E. H. *Identity: Youth and Crisis*. New York: Norton, 1968.

Erikson, Erik H., and Kai T. Erikson. "On the Confirmation of the Delinquent." *Chicago Review* 10 (1957): 15–23.

Evans, Ellis D., Judith Rutberg, Carmela Sather, et al. "Content Analysis of Contemporary Teen Magazines for Adolescent Females." *Youth and Society* 23 (1991): 99–120.

Ewen, Stuart. *Captains of Consciousness: Advertising and the Social Roots of the Consumer Culture*. New York: McGraw-Hill, 1976.

Fanon, Frantz. *The Wretched of the Earth*. New York: Grove Press, 1963.

Farnsworth, Dana L. "Adolescence: Terminable and Interminable." *Adolescent Psychiatry* 3 (1973): 31–43.

Farrell, Warren T. *The Liberated Man*. New York: Random House, 1974.

Feinstein, Sherman C. "Identity and Adjustment Disorders of Adolescence." *Comprehensive Textbook of Psychiatry*. 4th ed. Eds. Harold I. Kaplan and Benjamin J. Sadock. Baltimore: Williams and Wilkins, 1985. 1760–65.

Ferguson, Marjorie. *Forever Feminine: Women's Magazines and the Cult of Femininity*. London: Heinemann, 1983.

Fine, Gary A., Jeylan T. Mortimer and Donald F. Roberts. "Leisure, Work, and the Mass Media." *At the Threshold: The Developing Adolescent*. Eds. S. Shirley Feldman and Glen R. Elliott. Cambridge, MA: Harvard University Press, 1990. 225–52.

Forrest, T. R. "Such a Handsome Face: Advertising Male Cosmetics." *Feminist Frontiers II*. Eds. Laurel Richardson and Verta Taylor. New York: Random House, 1989.

Foucault, Michel. "Technologies of the Self: A Seminar with Michel Foucault." *Technologies of the Self*. Eds. Luther Martin, Huck Gutman, and Patrick Hutton. Amherst, MA: University of Massachusetts Press, 1988.

Franklin, Clyde W. "The Male Sex Drive." *Feminist Frontiers II.* Eds. Laurel Richardson and Verta Taylor. New York: Random House, 1989.

Freeman, Derek. *Margaret Mead and Samoa: The Making and Unmaking of an Anthropological Myth.* Cambridge, MA: Harvard University Press, 1983.

Gadpaille, Warren J. "Psychiatric Treatment of the Adolescent." *Comprehensive Textbook of Psychiatry.* Eds. Harold I. Kaplan and Benjamin J. Sadock. 4th ed. Baltimore: Williams and Wilkins, 1985.

Galambos, Nancy L., David M. Almeida and Anne C. Petersen. "Masculinity, Femininity, and Sex-Role Attitudes in Early Adolescence: Exploring Gender Intensification." *Child Development* 61 (1990): 1905–14.

Garmezy, Norman. "DSMIII. Never Mind the Psychologists: Is It Good for the Children?" *The Clinical Psychologist* 31 (1983): 4–6.

Gergen, Kenneth J. "The Decline of Personality." *Psychology Today* (November/December 1992): 59–63.

Gibson, Stacey. "University Degree May Lead to a Dead-End Job." *The* [UWO] *Gazette* (March 25, 1993): 1.

Gilbert, Sid. *Attrition in Canadian Universities.* Guelph, ON: Commission of Inquiry on Canadian University Education, 1991.

Gillis, John R. *Youth and History: Tradition and Change in European Age Relations: 1770–Present.* New York: Academic Press, 1974.

Giroux, Henry. *Curriculum Discourse as Postmodern Critical Practice.* Geelong, Australia: Deakin University Press, 1990.

Glasser, William. *The Identity Society.* New York: Harper and Row, 1972.

Goffman, Erving. "On Cooling Out the Mark: Some Aspects of Adaptation to Failure." *Psychiatry* 15 (1952): 451–63.

Graham, Lawrence, and Lawrence Hamdan. *Youthtrends: Capturing the $200 Billion Youth Market.* Toronto: McClelland and Stewart, 1989.

Green, Kenneth C., and Alexander Astin. "The Mood on Campus: More Conservative or Just More Materialistic?" *Educational Record* (Winter 1985): 45–48.

Hadenius, Stig, and Ann Lindgren. *On Sweden.* Stockholm: Swedish Institute, 1990.

Hagan, John, and Blair Wheaton. "The Search for Adolescent Role Exits and the Transition to Adulthood." *Social Forces* 71 (1993): 955–80.

Hall, G. Stanley. *Adolescence*. New York: Appleton, 1904.

Hare-Mustin, Rachel T., and Jeanne Marecek. "The Meaning of Difference: Gender Theory, Postmodernism, and Psychology." *American Psychologist* 43 (1988): 455–64.

Hargreaves, Andy, and Ivor Goodson. *Schools of the Future: Towards a Canadian Vision*. Ottawa: Innovations Program, Employment and Immigration Canada, 1992.

Harris, Marvin. "Margaret and the Giant-Killer." *The Sciences* 23 (1983): 18–21.

Haugen, Steven E., and Earl F. Mellor. "Estimating the Number of Minimum Wage Earners." *Monthly Labor Review* (January 1990): 70–74.

Hecker, Daniel E. "Reconciling Conflicting Data on Jobs for College Graduates." *Monthly Labor Review* (July 1992): 3–12.

Herdman, Roger C., and Clyde J. Behney. *Adolescent Health*. Washington: Office of Technology Assessment, 1991.

Herman, Edward S., and Noam Chomsky. *Manufacturing Consent: The Political Economy of the Mass Media*. New York: Pantheon, 1988.

Hess, Melanie. "Sinful Wages." *Perception: Canada's Social Development Magazine* 15.3 (1991): 29–32.

Hill, John P., and Mary Ellen Lynch. "The Intensification of Gender-Related Role Expectations During Early Adolescence." *Girls at Puberty: Biological and Psychological Perspectives*. Eds. Jeanne Brooks-Gunn and Anne C. Petersen. New York: Plenum, 1983.

Hill, Richard F., and J. Dennis Fortenberry. "Adolescence as a Culture-Bound Syndrome." *Social Science and Medicine* 35 (1992): 73–80.

Holmes, Janelle, and Eliane Leslau Silverman. *We're Here, Listen to Us! A Survey of Young Women in Canada*. Ottawa: Canadian Advisory Council on the Status of Women, 1992.

Howe, Neil, and Bill Strauss. *13th GEN: Abort, Retry, Ignore, Fail?* New York: Vintage Books, 1993.

Huston, Aletha C., and Mildred M. Alvarez. "The Socialization Context of Gender Role Development in Early Adoles-

cence." *Biology of Adolescent Behavior and Development*. Eds.
Gerald Adams, Raymond Montemayor, and Thomas P. Gullotta. Beverly Hills, CA: Sage, 1990.

Huxley, Aldous. *Brave New World*. London: Triad Grafton, 1932.

————. *Brave New World Revisited*. New York: Harper and
Row, 1958.

Jamsin, Gilles, and Ramona McDowell. *The Labour Market Experience of Social Science Graduates: The Class of 1982 Revisited*.
Ottawa: Department of the Secretary of State of Canada,
1989.

Jessor, Richard. "Risk Behavior in Adolescence: A Psychosocial
Framework for Understanding and Action." *Journal of Adolescent Health* 12 (1991): 597–605.

————. "Successful Adolescent Development Among Youth in
High-Risk Settings." *American Psychologist* 48 (1993): 117–26.

Kantrowitz, Barbara. "Wild in the Streets." *Newsweek* (August
2, 1993): 40–47.

Keniston, Kenneth. "Prologue: Youth as a Stage of Life." *Youth*.
Eds. Robert Havighurst and P. H. Dreyer. Chicago: University of Chicago Press, 1975.

Kett, Joseph F. *Rites of Passage*. New York: Basic, 1977.

Klein, Hugh. "Adolescence, Youth, and Young Adulthood:
Rethinking Current Conceptualizations of Life Stage." *Youth
and Society* 21 (1990): 446–71.

Komarovsky, Mirra. *Dilemmas of Masculinity*. New York: Norton, 1976.

Korenblum, Marshall. "Canada's Troubled Youth and the Real
Victim of Society?" *Globe and Mail* (March 24, 1986): A7.

Krahn, Harvey, and Graham Lowe. "Transitions to Work: Find-
ings from a Longitudinal Study of High-School and Univer-
sity Graduates in Three Canadian Cities." *Making their Way:
Education, Training and the Labour Market in Canada and Great
Britain*. Eds. David Ashton and Graham Lowe. Toronto:
University of Toronto Press, 1991.

Lengermann, Patricia Madoo, and Ruth A. Wallace. *Gender in
America: Social Control and Social Change*. Englewood
Cliffs, NJ: Prentice-Hall, 1985.

Levine, Saul. *Radical Departures: Desperate Detours to Growing Up*.
New York: Harcourt Brace Jovanovich, 1984.

Levitt, Cyril. *Children of Privilege: Student Revolt in the Sixties.* Toronto: University of Toronto Press, 1984.

Lifton, Robert J. "Protean Man." *Partisan Review* 35 (1968): 13–27.

Lindsay, Colin. "The Service Sector in the 1980s." *Canadian Social Trends* (Spring 1989): 20–23.

Lindsay, Linda L. *Gender Roles: A Sociological Perspective.* Englewood Cliffs, NJ: Prentice-Hall, 1990.

Livingstone, David W. "Lifelong Education and Chronic Underemployment: Exploring the Contradiction." *Transitions: Schooling and Employment in Canada.* Eds. Paul Anisef and Paul Axelrod. Toronto: Thompson Educational Publishing, 1993.

Lockhart, R. Alexander. "Graduate Unemployment and the Myth of Human Capital." *Social Space: Canadian Perspectives.* Eds. D. T. Davies and K. Herman. Toronto: New Press, 1971.

Lyman, Peter. "The Fraternal Bond as a Joking Relationship: A Case Study of the Role of Sexist Jokes in Male Group Bonding." *Changing Men.* Ed. Michael S. Kimmel. Beverly Hills, CA: Sage, 1987.

Mackie, Marlene. *Gender Relations in Canada: Further Explorations.* Toronto: Butterworths, 1991.

Mandell, Nancy, and Stewart Crysdale. "Gender Tracks: Male-Female Perceptions of Home-School-Work Transitions." *Transitions: Schooling and Employment in Canada.* Eds. Paul Anisef and Paul Axelrod. Toronto: Thompson Educational Publishing, 1993.

Manning, M. Lee. "Three Myths Concerning Adolescence." *Adolescence* 18 (1983): 823–20.

Marcia, James E. "Identity in Adolescence." *Handbook of Adolescent Psychology.* Ed. Joseph Adelson. New York: Wiley, 1980.

Marcuse, Herbert. *One-Dimensional Man.* Boston: Beacon Press, 1964.

———. *An Essay on Liberation.* Boston: Beacon Press, 1969.

———. *Counter-Revolution and Revolt.* Boston: Beacon Press, 1972.

Marney, Jo. "Teen Market Offers Growing Opportunities." *Marketing* (December 1991): 14.

Marx, Karl, and Friedrich Engels. *The German Ideology.* New York: International Publishers, 1969.

McCain, Garvin, and Erwin M. Segal. *The Game of Science*. Belmont, CA: Brooks/Cole, 1969.

McCulloch, Michael. "The Facts of Employment, 1990." *Perception: Canada's Social Development Magazine* 15 (1991): 17–19.

Mead, Margaret. *Coming of Age in Samoa: A Psychological Study of Primitive Youth for Western Civilization*. New York: Morrow Quill Paperbacks, 1928.

Melton, Gary B. "Rights of Adolescents." *Encyclopedia of Adolescence*, 930–933. Eds. Richard M. Lerner, Anne C. Petersen, and Jeanne Brooks-Gunn. New York: Garland, 1991.

Messner, Michael. "The Life of a Man's Seasons: Male Identity in the Life Course of the Jock." *Changing Men*. Ed. Michael S. Kimmel. Newbury Park, CA: Sage, 1987.

Millet, Kate. *Sexual Politics*. New York: Avon, 1971.

Mills, C. Wright. *The Sociological Imagination*. New York: Oxford University Press, 1959.

Mirel, Jeffrey E. "Twentieth-Century America, Adolescence in." *Encyclopedia of Adolescence*, 1153–58. Eds. Richard M. Lerner, Anne C. Petersen, and Jeanne Brooks-Gunn. New York: Garland, 1991.

Mongardini, Carlo. "The Ideology of Postmodernity." *Theory, Culture and Society* 9 (1992): 55-65.

Montemayor, Raymond, Gerald R. Adams and Thomas P. Gullotta, eds. *From Childhood to Adolescence: A Transitional Period?* Beverly Hills, CA: Sage, 1990.

Montemayor, Raymond, and Daniel J. Flannery. "Making the Transition from Childhood to Early Adolescence." *From Childhood to Adolescence: A Transitional Period?* Eds. Raymond Montemayor, Gerald R. Adams, and Thomas P. Gullotta. Beverly Hills, CA: Sage, 1990.

Muuss, Rolf E. *Theories of Adolescence*. 5th ed. New York: McGraw-Hill, 1988.

Myles, John. "The Expanding Middle: Some Canadian Evidence on the Deskilling Debate." *Canadian Review of Sociology and Anthropology* 25 (1988): 335–64.

Myles, John, W. G. Picot and Ted Wannell. *Wages and Jobs in the 1980s: Changing Youth Wages and the Declining Middle*. Ottawa: Statistics Canada, Social and Economic Studies Division, 1988.

Nava, Mica. *Changing Cultures: Feminism, Youth and Consumerism.* Newbury Park, CA: Sage, 1992.

Nielsen, Linda. *Adolescence: A Contemporary View.* 2nd ed. Fort Worth, Texas: Harcourt Brace Jovanovich, 1991.

Nobert, Lucie. *Profile of Highter Education in Canada: 1990 Edition.* Ottawa: Department of the Secretary of State, 1991.

Nobert, Lucie, Ramona McDowell and Diane Goulet. *Profile of Higher Education in Canada: 1991 Edition.* Ottawa: Department of the Secretary of State, 1992.

O'Neill, Jeff. "Changing Occupational Structure." *Canadian Social Trends* (Winter 1991): 8–12.

Oderkirk, Jillian. "Educational Achievement: An International Comparison." *Canadian Social Trends* (Autumn 1993): 8–12.

Offer, Daniel, and R. B. Church. "Adolescent Turmoil." *Encyclopedia of Adolescence*, 1148–1152. Eds. Richard M. Lerner, Anne C. Petersen, and Jeanne Brooks-Gunn. New York: Garland, 1991.

Offer, D., and J. B. Offer. *From Teenage to Young Manhood: A Psychological Study.* New York: Basic Books, 1975.

Offer, Daniel, and Melvin Sabshin. *Normality and the Life Cycle: A Critical Integration.* New York: Basic Books, 1984.

Organization for Economic Cooperation and Development (OECD). *Becoming Adult in a Changing Society.* Paris: OECD, 1985.

Orwell, George. *Nineteen Eighty-Four.* New York: Penguin, 1948.

Paikoff, Roberta L., and Jeanne Brooks-Gunn. "Physiological Processes: What Role Do They Play in the Transition to Adolescence?" *From Childhood to Adolescence: A Transitional Period? Advances in Adolescent Development.* Vol. 2. Eds. Raymond Montemayor, Gerald R. Adams, and Thomas P. Gullotta. Beverly Hills, CA: Sage, 1990.

Parliament, Jo-Anne B. "Labour Force Trends: Two Decades in Review." *Canadian Social Trends* (Autumn 1990): 16–19.

Petersen, Anne C., and Brandon Taylor. "The Biological Approach to Adolescence: Biological Change and Psychological Adaptation." *Handbook of Adolescent Psychology.* Ed. Joseph Adelson. New York: John Wiley and Sons, 1980.

Pomfret, Alan. "Education." *Introducton to Sociology: A Canadian Focus.* Ed. James J. Teevan. Scarborough, ON: Prentice-Hall, 1982.

Porter, John. "Education and the Just Society." *Sociology for Canadians: A Reader*. Eds. Alexander Himelfarb and C. James Richardson. Toronto: McGraw-Hill Ryerson, 1984.

Proefrock, David W. "Adolescence: Social Fact and Psychological Concept." *Adolescence* 26.64 (1981): 851–58.

Recascino-Wise, Lois, and Bjorn Jonzon. "Policies for Employing Young People." *Current Sweden* 371 (February). Stockholm: Swedish Institute, 1990.

Rejai, Mostafa. "Political Ideology: Theoretical and Comparative Perspectives." *Decline of Ideology*. Ed. Mostafa Rejai. Chicago: Aldine and Atherton, 1971.

Renzetti, Claire M., and Daniel J. Curran. *Women, Men, and Society*. Boston: Allyn and Bacon, 1992.

Richmond-Abbott, Marie. *Masculine and Feminine: Gender Roles over the Life Cycle*. 2nd ed. New York: McGraw-Hill, 1992.

Rinehart, James. *The Tyranny of Work*. Toronto: Academic Press, 1986.

Roazen, Paul. *Erik H. Erikson: The Power and Limits of a Vision*. New York: Free Press, 1976.

Rosenhan, D. L. "On Being Sane in Insane Places." *Science* 179 (1973): 250–58.

Ross, David P. "Action Needed on Education for Indians." *Perception: Canada's Social Development Magazine* (Fall/Winter 1992): 27-30.

Ross, David P., and Ross Shillington. *The Canadian Fact Book on Poverty, 1989*. Ottawa: Canadian Council on Social Development, 1990.

Rowe, David C., and Joseph Lee Rodgers. "Behavioral Genetics, Adolescence Deviance, and 'D': Contributions and Issues." *Biology of Adolescent Behavior and Development*. Eds. Gerald Adams, Raymond Montemayor, and Thomas P. Gullotta. Beverly Hills, CA: Sage, 1990.

Rowntree, John, and Margaret Rowntree. "The Political Economy of Youth." *Our Generation* 6 (1968): 155–90.

Sabo, Donald, and Sue Curry Janse. "Images of Men in Sport Media: The Social Reproduction of Gender Order." *Men, Masculinity, and the Media*. Ed. Steve Craig. Newbury Park, CA: Sage, 1992.

Sadker, Mirra, and David Sadker. "Sexism in the Classroom in the 1980s." *Psychology Today* (March 1985): 54–57.

Schultze, Quentin J., Roy M. Anker, James D. Bratt, et al. *Dancing in the Dark: Youth, Popular Culture, and the Electronic Media.* Grand Rapids, MI: William B. Eerdmans Publishing, 1990.

Seligman, Martin. "Boomer Blues." *Psychology Today* (October 1988): 50–55.

Sexton, Linda G. *Between Two Worlds: Young Women in Crisis.* New York: Morrow, 1979.

Shelley, Kristina J. "The Future of Jobs for College Graduates." *Monthly Labor Review* (July 1992): 13–21.

Sherif, Muzafer, O. J. Harvey, B. J. White, et al. *Intergroup Conflicted Co-operation: The Robber's Cave Experiment.* University of Oklahoma: Norman Institute of Group Relations, 1961.

Smart, Barry. *Postmodernity.* London: Routledge, 1993.

Sorrentino, Constance. "International Comparisons of Unemployment Indicators." *Monthly Labor Review* (March 1993): 3–15.

Spade, Joan Z., and Carole A. Reese. "We've Come a Long Way, Maybe: College Students' Plans for Work and Family." *Sex Roles* 24 (1991): 309–21.

Springhall, John. *Coming of Age: Adolescence in Britain 1860–1960.* Dublin: Gill and MacMillan, 1986.

Sprinthall, Norman A., and W. Andrew Collins. *Adolescent Psychology: A Developmental View.* Reading, MA: Addison-Wesley, 1984.

Stainby, Mia. "Boomerang Kids Surprise Parents in Return to Nest." *Peterborough Examiner* (January 5, 1993): B5.

Statistics Canada. *Youth in Canada: Selected Highlights.* Catalogue Number 89–511. Ottawa: Housing, Family and Social Statistics Division, 1989a.

Statistics Canada. *Health Reports.* Catalogue Number 82–003. Ottawa: Canadian Centre for Health Information, 1989b.

Steinberg, Laurence. "Bound to Bicker." *Psychology Today* (September 1987): 36–39.

—————. "Pubertal Maturation and Parent-Adolescent Distance: An Evolutionary Perspective." *Biology of Adolescent Behavior and Development.* Eds. Gerald R. Adams, Raymond Montemayor, and Thomas P. Gullotta. Beverly Hills, CA: Sage, 1990.

Stockard, Jean, and Miriam M. Johnson. *Sex and Gender in Society.* Englewood Cliffs, NJ: Prentice Hall, 1992.

Strang, Scott P., and Jacob L. Orlofsky. "Factors Underlying Suicidal Ideation Among College Students: A Test of Teicher and Jacob's Model." *Journal of Adolescence* 13 (1990): 39–52.

Sunter, Deborah. "School, Work, and Dropping Out." *Perspectives on Labour and Income* (Summer 1993): 44–52.

Susman, Elizabeth J., and Lorah D. Dorn. "Hormones and Behavior in Adolescence." *Encyclopedia of Adolescence*, 513–17. Eds. Richard M. Lerner, Anne C. Petersen, and Jeanne Brooks-Gunn. New York: Garland, 1991.

Swedish Institute. *Fact Sheets on Sweden: Facts and Figures About Youth in Sweden.* Stockholm: Swedish Institute, 1991.

Swedish Institute. *Higher Education in Sweden.* Stockholm: Swedish Institute, 1992.

Tait, Gordon. "Youth, Personhood and 'Practices of the Self': Some New Directions for Youth Research." *Australia and New Zealand Journal of Sociology* 29 (1993): 40–54.

Tinning, R. Richard, and Lindsay Fitzclarence. "Postmodern Youth Culture and the Crisis in Australian Secondary School Physical Education." *Quest* 44 (1992): 287–303.

U.S. Department of Commerce. *Statistical Abstracts of the United States 1991.* Washington: U.S. Department of Commerce, 1991.

Udry, J. Richard. "Adolescent Problem Behavior." *Social Biology* 37 (1990): 1–10.

Wannell, Ted. "Losing Ground: Wages of Young People, 1981–1986." *Canadian Social Trends* (Summer 1989): 21–23.

William T. Grant Foundation. *The Forgotten Half: Non-College Youth in America.* Washington: William T. Grant Foundation, 1988.

Winnicott, D. W. "Adolescence: Struggling Through the Doldrums." *Adolescent Psychiatry* 1 (1971): 40–51.

Wrong, Dennis. "The Over-Socialized Conception of Man in Modern Sociology." *American Sociological Review* 2 (1961): 188–92.

York, Geoffrey. "Crime Is Ticket to Escape Northern Woes." *Globe and Mail* (October 26, 1987): A1, A4.

# Index

force, for social control, 141
Fortenberry, J. Dennis, 9–10
Foucault, Michel, 23
fraternities, 123
free enterprise, and university
    education, 123
free household labor, 96
free world, 113–14
freedom, 115, 117, 142–3
Freud, Anna, 71
Freud, Sigmund, 71, 72
full employment, 155–6
functionalism, 16–20, 26

**G**
Gadpaille, Warren, 10
gangs, 118
    armed, 150
    Los Angeles, 183–4
Garmezy, Norman, 11
gender, 86
    attitudes in Western societies,
      86
    as big business, 85
    and biological differences, 85
    and college participation, 77
    comparisons, 85
    conditioning, 95
    discrimination, 168
    equality, 88–9
    and job success, 39
    male stereotype, 94
    and power, 66
    tracking, 179
    use of term, 179
gender differences, 23–5, 88
    advanced industrial nations,
      34

earning power, 49–50
and socialization factors, 84
television content, 92
gender intensification, 84–95
    and coming of age, 95–100
    and young men, 93–5
genetics and cultural evolution,
    168
ghettoization, occupational, 67
Giroux, Henry, 22
*Glamour* magazine, 147
glass ceiling, 98
globalization, 22, 33, 136
Goffman, Erving, 170
Goodson, Ivor, 41, 137–8
Gorbachev, Mikhail, 113
government policies:
    economy, 68
    and poverty, 57
    and youth, 151–2
government-sponsored
    programs (U.S.), 162
graduates, surveys of, 37–9,
    43–4
Graham, Lawrence, 119
Great Britain, 143
    and youth study, 23–4
Grey Cup, 139
guidance counselors, 88
Gulf War *see* Persian Gulf War

**H**
Hadenius, Stig, 158
Hall, G. Stanley, 5, 6, 7
Hamdan , Lawrence, 119
Hargreaves, Andy, 41, 137–8
Harris, Marvin, 168
Hecker, Daniel, 38

helping professions, mandate
of, 10–11
Herman, Edward, 105–6
high-school, 161
degrees, 121
drop-out rate, 40–4, 79, 160
truancy, 138–9
High-school and college
enrollments in the United
States over the past
century (Table), 35
high-technology economy, 17
higher education, and the
workplace, 37
Hill, Robert, 9–10
Hispanic gangs, 118
homemakers, 96
homicide, among racial
minorities, 64
homogenization of women, 87
hormone levels theory, 14, 61
humanistic values, 162
Hussein, Saddam, 113, 116
Huston, Aletha, 89, 92
Huxley, Aldous, 68, 109, 130–2
social control model, 132–3

## I

identity:
disorder, 12
manipulation, 80–3, 86, 95, 99
moratorium, 74, 76, 164
society, 82
theory, 71
identity confusion:
and perpetual adolescence, 83
and social environment, 160
identity crisis, 75
and aging process, 97

and culture, 70
exigencies of war, 73
gender differences, 97–8
identity-forming industries, 68
ideology:
as body of beliefs, 110–11
as body of ideas, 110–11
and class, 117
in contemporary society,
131–2
and control, 130, 132
of freedom, 142–3
of gender, 84–5
and illusion, 115–16
and language, 111–12
and power, 117
of treatment, 11
of youth, 107–11, 120–8, 160
illiteracy, 137–8
illusion, and ideology, 115–16
incompletion rate, at university,
43
independence from parents,
52–3
Indian children see native people
Indians, non-status, 80
individual, focus on, 6–7
individualism, 62, 134
Indoctrination into con-
sumerism? (Chart), 149
industrial capitalism, 151, 159
workplace, 96
Industrial Revolution, 120
industrialization, 16–20, 32
and the nuclear family, 85
and view of youth, 108–9
information economy, 17
information technologies, 22,
136